MAKE MONEY

AS

A BUYER'S AGENT

Double Your Commissions by Working with Real Estate Buyers

CHANTAL HOWELL CAREY
BILL CAREY

John Wiley & Sons, Inc.

**With love to all our family, friends, and dedicated students!
May you always have more blessings than you need!**

Published by John Wiley & Sons, Inc., Hoboken, New Jersey.
Published simultaneously in Canada.

For general information on our other products and services or for technical support, please
contact our Customer Care Department within the United States at (800) 762-2974, outside
the United States at (317) 572-3993 or fax (317) 572-4002.

Wiley also publishes its books in a variety of electronic formats. Some content that appears in
print may not be available in electronic books. For more information about Wiley products,
visit our web site at www.wiley.com.

Library of Congress Cataloging-in-Publication Data:
Howell-Carey, Chantal.
    Make money as a buyer's agent : double your commissions by working with real
estate buyers / Chantal Howell Carey, Bill Carey.
      p. cm.
    Includes index.
    ISBN 978-0-470-05125-2 (cloth)
  1. Real estate agents—United States. 2. Real estate business—United States.
    3. Agency (Law)—United States. I. Carey, Bill, 1951– II. Title.
    HD278.H68 2007
    333.33068—dc22   2006030748

Printed in the United States of America.
10 9 8 7 6 5 4 3 2 1

CONTENTS

PREFACE

M any of you have made huge profits over the last five years as your real estate business has enjoyed unprecedented success. The residential resale market has enjoyed historic activity over this time period. The year 2004 led the way as the number one resale market of all time. The year 2005 came in a close second. And for all the gloom and doom from the media during the past year, 2006 came in third.

The key to your success was listing sellers. It was a seller's market. As soon as you put the for sale sign in the front yard, it seemed like you had three offers that day. Many times the successful offer was for higher than the original listing price! The seller was happy and you were happy.

Several forces drove this seller's market. They included the technology and stock market crash of 2000, which drove investment dollars into real estate. Another force was historically low interest rates as the Federal Reserve battled the effects of 9/11 and economic recession. A third force was the movement of the real estate cycle from the recession/depression phase into the expansion/prosperity phase.

Normal Real Estate Market

We are now in a normal real estate market. It is no longer a seller's market. We define a normal real estate market as striking a balance between sellers and buyers. It is neither a seller's market nor a buyer's market. We know that you have noticed that it is still relatively easy for you to list sellers. It has become relatively harder for you to find buyers to buy your seller listings. Buyers are out there, however, and they are buying real estate.

The question you have to ask yourself is what is the most efficient and profitable way to work with buyers in a normal real estate market? We invite you to throw out everything you know about working with buyers in a seller's market. None of that will work in a normal real estate market. Let's look at the current paradigm of the real estate industry with regard to working with buyers.

The Current Paradigm of the Real Estate Industry

Have you ever lost a buyer to an open house? How about losing a buyer to new home construction? Have you ever lost a buyer to a for sale by owner? How about losing a buyer to another real estate licensee? If you have been in the real estate business for any period of time—two weeks, two months, or two years—you have had the unpleasant experience of losing buyers with whom you have worked.

The current paradigm of the real estate industry requires that you work for free when you work with buyers. At best, this paradigm requires that you work for many hours before you are compensated. And you may have to work with 10 buyers to make one sale. Why do you accept working within this paradigm? What is the solution?

The Real Estate Profession Today

Today, as a real estate professional, you are confronted with ongoing and necessary education requirements. These education requirements must be fulfilled by you in a timely manner or you will lose your real estate license. Every year, you are required to take on more responsibility in the areas of consumer protection, professional ethics, and financial knowledge.

Liability

As a real estate professional, you are liable for everything you do and say when you are engaged in your real estate business.

These are acts of commission. You are also liable for everything you do not do and do not say when you are engaged in your real estate business. These are acts of omission.

Right now, you are taking actions or not taking actions in your real estate business that you may feel are completely honest, ethical, and professional. These actions or inactions you are taking today are the actions or inactions you are going to be sued for in the next three to five years.

You Are Worth the Money

Every one of you reading this book has no qualms about asking a seller to sign an exclusive authorization and right-to-sell listing agreement. In fact, if the seller will not sign the listing agreement, you will not take on the liability of being their agent or wasting your time and money marketing their property.

You also have no qualms about asking the seller to agree to pay you or your company a commission of 6 percent to 7 percent of the selling price. You are paid this commission if anyone, including the seller, brings a buyer who buys the property. With the average selling price of real estate in the United States approaching $300,000, the average real estate commission is in the $18,000 to $21,000 range.

6% Real Estate Commission

Average Selling Price	$300,000
Real Estate Commission Percentage	× 6%
Real Estate Commission	$18,000

7% Real Estate Commission

Average Selling Price	$300,000
Real Estate Commission Percentage	× 7%
Real Estate Commission	$21,000

We know in your paradigm of working with buyers that you have many qualms about asking a buyer to agree to pay you or your company a real estate commission. If you are working with a buyer who is looking for the average price home of $300,000, $18,000 to $21,000 of real estate commissions are on the table.

How are you going to get your share? And why are you willing to risk the loss of this much money by working without a written agreement with the buyer? By the way, you are also liable for your acts of commission and omission when you work with a buyer. In your paradigm of working with buyers, you have all the liability of working with sellers but with no guarantee of compensation.

Who We Are

In 1985, Chantal began requiring buyers to deposit their earnest money with her company, CH International Realty in Dallas, Texas, before she would agree to work with them. She would put this money in her broker's trust account. Now she knew they were serious about buying. In Texas, you put your money where your mouth is.

In 1986, Bill and his partner started Real Estate Buyer's Service in San Diego, California. This company listed and worked exclusively with buyers. The buyer was required to pay a nonrefundable retainer of one-half of 1 percent (0.5%) of the upper limit of the purchase price to Real Estate Buyer's Service before Bill or his partner would work with them.

If a buyer was looking at a $300,000 upper limit purchase price, the nonrefundable retainer would be $1,500. Have we got your attention?

Nonrefundable Retainer

Upper Limit Purchase Price	$300,000
Percentage of Retainer	× 0.5%
Retainer Amount	$1,500

We Are Here to Revolutionize Your Real Estate Business

This book will revolutionize your real estate business. We are going to give you all the tools necessary to design a new paradigm for working with buyers. In fact, we boldly predict that you will double your commissions working with buyers once you start operating out of this new paradigm. And you will never work with buyers for free again!

We are passionate about professionalizing the real estate industry in working with buyers. We are presenting the most advanced material available in residential real estate. We dedicate this book to you whether you are a one-person brokerage or the head of a national real estate company, whether you are a beginning salesperson or an experienced professional, whether you are making tons of money with buyers or have sworn off working with buyers forever.

Good luck and good reading.

Chantal & Bill Carey

INTRODUCTION

Over the years, we have traveled throughout the country teaching real estate, financial, motivational, and interpersonal skills seminars to our students. We are always striving to be on the leading edge.

Regarding real estate, we have taught everything from buying and selling it creatively as an individual or an investor to core classes for licensing and passing real estate broker's exams. Just about anything you can think of related to real estate we have taught to someone somewhere!

With a new market comes new ideas. We have distilled the knowledge and experience we have gained from buying and selling real estate for ourselves and our clients and helping our students over the last three decades.

Make Money as a Buyer's Agent: Double Your Commissions by Working with Real Estate Buyers is the 11th real estate book we have written. Our first book, *How to Sell Your Home Without a Broker,* is in its fourth edition (Hoboken, NJ: Wiley, 2004). Robert J. Bruss, a nationally syndicated real estate columnist, said, "On a scale of 1 to 10 this book rates a 10."

Our fifth book, *Going Going Gone! Auctioning Your Home for Top Dollar* (Hoboken, NJ: Wiley, 2001), was also written to benefit the home owner in the selling of a home. Like *How to Sell Your Home Without a Broker,* our auctioning book was designed to show you how to successfully sell your home and net the most money.

Our sixth book, *The New Path to Real Estate Wealth: Earning Without Owning* (Hoboken, NJ: Wiley, 2004), was the first book in our new series designed specifically for active real estate investors. Our Win Going In! series is designed to take you from being a novice real estate investor to being an expert real estate investor.

The New Path to Real Estate Wealth: Earning Without Owning takes you from the real estate basics through the four best ways to make money in real estate. From flipping property to assigning contracts to controlling property using options to buying discount mortgage paper, it teaches you everything you need to know to become a successful real estate investor. In all four areas, we train you how to make money without buying or owning property!

Our premise for the Win Going In! series is that no matter what kind of real estate investment you are going to make, you have to win going in. It is no longer enough to make money on the back end of a deal or make a profit when you get out of a deal. The deal must have a profit built in on the front end, or else you shouldn't do it at all.

Our seventh book, *Quick Cash in Foreclosures* (Hoboken, NJ: Wiley, 2004), was the second book in our Win Going In! series. Robert J. Bruss picked this book as one of his top 10 real estate books of 2004. In it, we show you how to make money going into a foreclosure deal. It is a hands-on book that teaches you how to enter the real estate foreclosure market and make deals happen. What is unique about the book is that we show you how to have a quick cash investment strategy that you can successfully implement with little or no investment capital.

Our philosophy is that if you can be active in your investment life, you need to be in control of your investments. Counting on a stock broker, investment adviser, accountant, general partner, or real estate investment fund leaves you completely out of control. When you are an active real estate investor, you are the one calling the shots. You are the one responsible for your successes and failures.

Our eighth book, *Make Money in Real Estate Tax Liens: How to Guarantee Returns Up to 50%* (Hoboken, NJ: Wiley, 2005), was the third book in the Win Going In! series. In it, we teach you how to make money investing in real estate tax liens. Once a real estate tax lien is placed against real property, one of two things will happen.

Either the lien will be paid off by the owner of the property or an investor will buy the lien from the taxing agency that filed it. If the owner of the property does not redeem the lien from the investor, the investor can foreclose on the property and gain an ownership interest.

By investing in real estate tax liens, for pennies on the dollar, you can control a property. Your guarantee is you have the power of foreclosure in the event you are not paid back your original tax lien investment plus hefty interest and penalties. Investing in real estate tax liens is definitely a win going in!

Our ninth book, *Make Money in Short-Sale Foreclosures: How to Bypass Owners and Buy Directly from Lenders* (Hoboken, NJ: Wiley, 2006), was the fourth book in the Win Going In! series. In it, we teach you how to make money investing in short-sale foreclosures.

A short-sale foreclosure is a mortgage lender accepting less for the loan balance due as a payoff for the loan. Typically, loans are made for no more than 80 percent of the value of the property. In a short-sale, you are buying the property for less than the loan amount. This is buying real estate at a wholesale price.

By investing in short-sale foreclosures, you can bypass the owners and buy directly from the lenders. You can do this before, during, or after the foreclosure sale. Whichever way you choose to become involved and invest in short-sale foreclosures, you can make money.

Our tenth book, *Make Money in Abandoned Properties: How to Identify and Buy Vacant Properties and Make a Huge Profit* (Hoboken, NJ: Wiley, 2006), was the fifth book in the Win Going In! series. In it, we teach you how to make money investing in abandoned properties.

Owners abandon properties for three main reasons. These include financial reasons, death or divorce, and when the property becomes uninhabitable. Whatever the reasons, there is an opportunity for you to make money.

By investing in abandoned properties, you can buy real estate at wholesale prices. We show you how to locate the owners who have abandoned the properties and write a foolproof offer. We show you how to obtain financing to hold or rehab the property.

Make Money as a Buyer's Agent: Double Your Commissions by Working with Real Estate Buyers is our first book in our Make Money with Your Real Estate License series. Our purpose for the Make Money with Your Real Estate License series is to teach you all of our real estate knowledge and expertise.

We want to be the Brain Trust for your successful real estate industry career. The concepts in this book, as in all of our books, are applicable to most types of real estate industry practices just about anywhere. Now is the time for us in the real estate industry to shift our paradigm working with buyers and sellers.

We would love to hear from you about your successes listing buyers. We want to hear what is working and what is not working for you. We are available on a consulting basis to help you develop and implement your company policy working with buyers in the new paradigm. We also offer various real estate educational and investment programs.

On the investment side, we are available to help you put your deals together. We are available to partner deals. Please e-mail us at thetrustee@hotmail.com or contact us through our publisher, John Wiley & Sons. Good luck and congratulations on your success working with buyers!

Chantal & Bill Carey

CHAPTER 1

The History of the Real Estate Industry

The real estate industry of one hundred years ago looked very different than the real estate industry of today. Actually, in 1907 the real estate industry was not an industry at all. Similar to the town barber also being the person who pulled a rotten tooth (the forerunner of your friendly neighborhood dentist), the men who sold insurance were your friendly neighborhood real estate agents.

In some places even today, you can drive down the main street of a small town and see two or three businesses with signs that say "Insurance and Real Estate." Some of you reading this book are associated with very large real estate companies that have come full circle. These companies have returned to the historical linkage of insurance and real estate by offering a full range of financial services along with real estate services, such as Prudential Real Estate, among others.

For Sale by Owner

If the truth be told, back in the day, most real estate was bought and sold principal to principal without the assistance of a real estate industry. A seller would put a sign on their land, farm, store, commercial building, or home. The sign would say something like the following:

40 Acres Prime Grazing Land
$1000 Paper Money or $975 in Gold
See Fred at Moncrief's Feed Store

If you were a buyer interested in 40 acres of prime grazing land, you would go see Fred at the feed store. The negotiations would consist of you and Fred agreeing on the price and the terms, shaking hands, you giving Fred the money for the property, and then going to the clerk at the courthouse to have Fred sign a deed transferring the title to the property to you.

If you were smart, you would have Fred's signature witnessed by two people. This would add to the validity of the deed. Unfortunately, the witnesses more than likely would sign with an "X" because they could not read or write! Then you could ask the clerk of the court to record the deed in the courthouse records. After the deed was signed by Fred, you were the new owner of the property. Or were you?

Attorney's Opinion of Title

As for getting title insurance, there was no title insurance. At best, you could pay a local attorney to abstract the title. This would consist of the attorney looking at the existing recorded deeds at the courthouse. Then the attorney would give you a written opinion that Fred owned the acreage. This implied that you were receiving a valid deed from Fred giving you ownership of the property.

Many of you have heard the story of the famous American whose father purchased and lost three different properties based on initially receiving an attorney's opinion that he would receive valid title. Ownership claims were put forth by other parties on each property and in each instance were upheld by a court leading to the loss of all three properties.

The attorney's opinion of title was not worth the paper it was written on. Yes, you could sue the attorney, but what is the likelihood that the attorney had any money, or if they did, that you could get any of it? This happened to Abraham Lincoln's father for those of you who have not heard the story.

Sophisticated Marketing

If Fred was a savvy businessman, he might even place a classified ad in the town newspaper to advertise his acreage. The newspaper ad would read exactly the same as the sign on the property. If Fred owned property on the frontier, he might advertise in an eastern big-city newspaper to take advantage of the latest wave of immigrants chasing the American dream. This is how the ad might read in the *Chicago Sun:*

> 40 Acres Prime Grazing Land
> Where the West Begins
> $1000 Paper Money or $975 in Gold
> Write or Telegraph to Fred Moncrief, Fort Worth, Texas

The Real Estate Business in 1907

Let's say you were one of the people in Fort Worth who sold insurance and real estate in 1907. You see Fred's ad in the *Fort Worth Star* newspaper. As a smart businessman, you decide to go pay Fred a visit at the feed store. You have a client coming in from Chicago in the next week who would be interested in Fred's 40 acres.

You would really like to get Fred's insurance business. Fred is one of the up-and-coming movers and shakers in the business community. Besides the feed store, the Moncrief family owns one of the slaughterhouses that sends beef north and east to satisfy the insatiable American hunger for meat. Perhaps you can get on Fred's good side if you bring him a buyer for his grazing land.

You already have made a deal with the buyer from Chicago. If you find him something he likes, he has agreed to pay you $50 in gold. You know the buyer has $1,000 in gold to spend on Texas grazing land and pay you your fee. If you can negotiate the price of Fred's acreage down to $950 in gold, your buyer will have $50 in gold to pay you.

Deal or No Deal

You meet with Fred at the feed store. You tell him you have a buyer from Chicago who is looking for exactly the property Fred has for sale and will pay in gold. You ask Fred if he will take $950 in gold for the property. Fred tells you he wants $975 in gold for the property or $1,000 in paper money; otherwise there will be no deal. (Does this sound like something you have heard from a seller before? The seller wants their price and their terms.)

You do some quick thinking on your feet. You know the acreage will be perfect for your Chicago client. With the $1,000 in gold from them, you can get Fred the $975 in gold he wants for the acreage. This will leave $25 in gold for your fee. This is not the $50 in gold you were expecting to receive.

Your hope is that Fred will want to send some of his insurance business your way now that you have demonstrated an ability to get him what he wanted for one of his real estate holdings. You are investing the $25 you are not receiving on the real estate side of your business to create client loyalty with Fred. This may lead to doing business with Fred in the future on both the insurance side and the real estate side. Amazingly, even at the beginning, real estate commissions were negotiable!

Soft Money versus Hard Money

We are sure some of you are wondering about the difference in price for Fred's acreage between paper money and gold. Real estate has always been a real asset. You can see it, hear it, touch it, smell it, and taste it. People form an emotional attachment to their real property.

Gold is also a real asset. People would bite a gold coin to see if it was real. They were biting it to discover if it was soft. Real gold is soft enough for your teeth to make an impression. One hundred years ago, people wanted to receive like kind property when they sold or traded one of their real assets. Gold for real estate or real estate for gold was like kind property.

Greenbacks

Paper money was highly suspect to most people. It was not a tangible asset. It was not real. In an effort to have people accept paper money in lieu of gold or silver and use it in everyday transactions, the federal government printed so-called greenbacks that were huge in size. Our money today is six inches by two and a half inches (6" × 2.5"). One hundred years ago, greenbacks were eight and a half inches by three and a half inches (8.5" × 3.5")!

Greenbacks also stated on the bill that they were redeemable for gold or silver by the federal government. The idea was that because of their sheer size and the fact that the U.S. government would guarantee the greenbacks with gold or silver, people would be more likely to use and accept paper money.

Fred wanted a risk premium for accepting paper money for his real estate. That is why he wanted $1,000 in paper money and only $975 in gold for the acreage. We have the expression "cash is king" in the real estate industry from these earliest origins. Cash then meant gold or silver. Paper money was not considered cash. Paper money was a promissory note that was considered inherently risky.

Open Listings for Sellers

What was your alternative to approaching Fred in 1907 if you didn't yet have the buyer from Chicago? Said another way, how could you convince Fred to list his 40 acres of prime grazing land with you? That was a piece of cake. Fred would give you a listing just for the asking. Just like Fred would give a listing for the asking to the other twenty to thirty people who were in the real estate business in Fort Worth with you at that time.

That's right. You could get an open listing from Fred. Fred might make an agreement with you to pay you a fee for bringing him a buyer who bought the property. You could put your real estate for sale sign on Fred's property. Of course any potential buyer might have a hard time distinguishing your real estate company's for sale sign from the other twenty or thirty real estate companies for sale signs that were also on Fred's property.

30 Different Real Estate Companies Signs

We know that for some of you picturing Fred's property with 30 different companies' real estate signs must look like something straight out of a Tim Burton nightmare movie. But that is the way business was done. The seller would agree to pay a fee only to the real estate salesperson who brought an accepted offer.

Or the seller could say, like Fred, that he wanted a net amount for his property and would not agree to pay any fee to you for bringing the buyer. The real estate agent would have to get paid by the buyer. Whatever amount you received from the buyer as your fee was between you and the buyer. The seller had no say-so in the matter.

No Exclusive Authorization and Right-to-Sell Listings

In 1907 there were no exclusive authorization and right-to-sell listings! Can you possibly imagine a real estate industry that looked and functioned like that? The point is that there was no real estate industry yet. There were insurance businesses that had a real estate fourth-cousin branch of the family.

No one was representing the seller. No one was representing the buyer. The seller was pitted against the buyer and the real estate agent. The buyer was pitted against the seller and the real estate agent. The real estate agent was pitted against the seller and the buyer.

The real estate business was literally every man for himself. And, as with many businesses of the time, women were few and far between in the real estate business. There was room for all kinds of shenanigans. At this point in time, the real estate business was completely unprofessional.

One Real Estate Agent and One Seller

By the 1920s, the real estate industry had emerged in the form that we recognize today. One real estate agent working for one seller became the standard. This was the breakthrough that put real estate on the map as an industry. One real estate agent working exclusively for the seller is in the seller's best interest. This professionalized half of the real estate industry.

Working with Sellers in Today's Real Estate Market

The way you work with sellers in today's real estate market has been developed over more than eighty years of real estate industry growth. Whether you work for a small company or a large company, the way you work with sellers is the same. In fact, the way you interact with sellers is automatic.

Every one of you works with sellers in the following manner. We will start with the assumption that you already have an appointment to make a listing presentation. After you have made your successful listing presentation, you will do the following over the next several days and weeks to market this property.

Lockbox and Pole Sign

You will put a lockbox on the property with a key from the seller to gain access to the property when the seller is not at home. You will order a pole sign to be placed in the front yard. You will input the data on the property to your local Multiple Listing Service using your desktop or laptop computer to expose the property to the other real estate agents in your area.

You will talk to your office manager about running ads for the property in the local newspapers. You will schedule the property for your office to caravan or preview. You may have even taken digital photos and made them available to prospective buyers or other agents on the Internet.

As part of your listing presentation, you have promised the seller several open houses that you will have your assistant schedule over the next two to three weeks. A flyer describing the property will be put in the flyer box on the real estate sign in the next two to three days. You have a buyer coming in from out of town next weekend who may find this property a perfect fit for their housing needs.

Exclusive Authorization and Right to Sell

And of course you will do all of this only after you have a written agreement signed between you and the seller. This exclusive authorization and right-to-sell agreement guarantees you will be compensated for services rendered to the seller. You do not even have to sell the property yourself.

As the listing agent, you or your company will earn the listing office commission no matter who sells the property. Someone in your office could bring the buyer. Someone from an office across town could bring the buyer. Someone from out of town could bring the buyer. Even the seller could bring the buyer and you would still earn your listing commission!

Is there any one of you out there who would do all the things you do to successfully market a property without a written and signed exclusive authorization and right-to-sell agreement between you and the seller? We know your answer. But how do you work with buyers?

Many Real Estate Agents and One Buyer

By the 1970s, the way the real estate industry worked with buyers had evolved into the form that we recognize today. Many real estate agents working with one buyer became the standard. This was the drawback that kept real estate from losing its fourth-cousin status as an industry. Many real estate agents working with one buyer is not in either the buyer's best interest or the many real estate agents' best interest. Working with buyers has remained unprofessional and needs a set of standards to professionalize this side of the business.

Working with Buyers in Today's Real Estate Market

The way you work with buyers in today's real estate market also has been developed over more than eighty years of real estate industry growth. Whether you work for a small company or a large company, the way you work with buyers is the same. In fact the way you interact with buyers, like the way you work with sellers, is also automatic.

Let's say you are in the office on the up desk on a Sunday morning. The phone rings and you have an interested buyer calling about your new listing. They have seen your ad in the Sunday paper. Your ad is one of 20 properties that they have circled as having potential. Then they have gone on the Internet and eliminated 10 of those potential properties.

They have time to look at three properties Sunday afternoon. They want to be home before the game starts. They are calling to eliminate 7 of the 10 remaining properties that they have picked out of the paper. This potential buyer is calling to eliminate your property over the phone!

Phone Wars

Congratulations, because you are an expert on the phone, you are able to convince the caller to come into your office. They will be there in one hour. You call and make an appointment with the seller to show the buyer the property. You already have defied the odds and are one of the three properties the buyer will take the time to see.

You know that once you get in front of the buyer, you will be able to sell them a piece of property. You are that good. However, you are already operating with one hand tied behind your back. This buyer is smart, sophisticated, and has been programmed to treat you as completely subservient. You disagree? Let's see how your meeting with the buyer turns out.

Meeting with the Buyer

You spend the next hour preparing to show the buyer your listing and three other properties that are listed with other brokers and that meet the buyer's requirements. You are feeling time pressure because the buyer has told you they do not have much time because they want to be at home to watch the game within two hours of meeting with you.

Within five minutes of the buyer arriving at your office, you put them in your car and begin driving them all over town. (Who did you say is paying for gas?) You show them your listing first. This will get you brownie points with your seller. This will turn out to be the high point of the day.

In between showing them the other three properties, you stop and buy everyone refreshments in order to provide them a good service experience. You are also building rapport and trying to discover how motivated the buyer is. Because you are so organized, you are able to show them all four properties and get them back to your office with plenty of time to spare for them to get home to watch the game.

You are feeling pretty good about yourself. You think you may have a live buyer on your hands this time. They really seemed to like your listing and one of the other properties you showed them. They seemed committed to you. They also seemed like they were ready to buy.

Although you have told yourself a million times not to do this, you cannot help but think about how much commission you will make if the buyer buys your listing. Even if they buy the other broker's listing, you will still make a nice commission.

The Follow-Up

Two or three days go by and you decide to follow up with your Sunday buyer. You have done more research and have found six more properties that may work for them. You call them on the phone and discover one more time why you hate working with buyers.

In the most pleased and excited tone, the buyer tells you that they have made an offer on one of the properties you showed them on Sunday and it has been accepted by the seller! You can hear in their voice that they expect you to be happy for them. After all, you have been so nice to them that they think you are one of their buddies. Of course, you feel like you have just been punched in the stomach. You are having a hard time breathing let alone saying anything.

You manage to recover enough to ask them what happened. They tell you that they called the listing agent on the other property you showed them that they liked and went back to see it after the game on Sunday. It was a tough choice for them between your listing and this other property.

The listing agent for the other property convinced them to write an offer and see if the seller would take it. Much to their surprise, what do you know the seller accepted their offer! Isn't that unbelievable? You numbly congratulate them and hang up the phone.

Time and Money Wasted

You have wasted your time, spent money on gas and refreshments, and made no money. Why did this happen to you?

Why does this keep happening to you? Maybe the buyer did not like you. Maybe the buyer felt you were too aggressive. Maybe you talked too much and should have listened more. We know why this happened to you. You did not have a professional relationship with the buyer.

The Real Estate Industry Paradigm for Buyers

The real estate industry paradigm for buyers historically is that buyers come in one of three categories. These categories are the real estate industry shoptalk that is not meant for public conversation. Category 1 is that buyers are liars. Category 2 is that buyers are flakes. Category 3 is that buyers are lookie-loos.

Category 1, buyers are liars, has been proved to you over and over. Buyers tell you that they are going to buy something but do not. Buyers tell you that they are going to buy property from you but then buy it from someone else. Buyers tell you they are motivated but are not motivated. Buyers tell you that they have a great credit score but, well, you know the answer.

Category 2, buyers are flakes, is one of the universal truths in the real estate industry. Buyers blow into your office bragging that they are going to buy this property and that property and a third property. They tell you that if you can find them good deals, they are going to make you lots of money. Just stick with them and you will have a lifelong business relationship. Yeah, right. This happens with one out of a hundred buyers.

Category 3, buyers are lookie-loos, is one of our all-time favorite buyer paradigms. Several years ago, a well-known real estate company produced a national TV commercial that was designed to show that they were professional when it came to taking care of the sellers that listed their properties with them. The implication was that unlike other companies, the company producing the ad would never let your home be overrun with lookie-loos.

Lookie-loos were portrayed in the ad as little cartoon characters that would just race through the seller's home with no intention of buying. The lookie-loos were just busy being nosey. They were unqualified buyers. The implication was that other companies would parade lookie-loos through a property to make the seller think they were actually working hard to sell the property. But they were just wasting the seller's and everyone else's time, including their own.

Only Sellers Are Worthy of Your Representation

The bottom line is that your paradigm regarding buyers is completely shaped by your thinking that only sellers are worthy of your representation. The reason buyers are liars, flakes, and lookie-loos is because of the way the real estate industry regards buyers. The real estate industry interacts with buyers with an open-listing mentality.

Many real estate agents working with one buyer is the norm for the real estate profession. Essentially, the real estate industry operates with buyers as open listings. An open listing with buyers means whatever agent sells the buyer a property gets a commission. Too bad for you if you showed the buyer the property first.

Buyers Are the True Consumers

Buyers are the true consumers in the real estate industry. You can have all kinds of exclusive authorization and right-to-sell listings with sellers. But until you have a buyer that is ready, willing, and able to purchase a piece of real property, you will not make one dime in real estate commissions.

Buyers are now demanding representation by real estate agents. Buyers realize they are the driving force of the real estate market. If you do not give a buyer complete representation in the real estate transaction, then they will find someone who will.

After all, a real estate purchase is the biggest ticket item that a consumer will make in their lifetime. That is until the next time they make a real estate purchase! If we do not represent buyers, someone else will. We are not kidding about this. Attorneys are very interested in working with buyers.

In the next chapter, we will talk about the changing real estate market. We are in the process of going from open listings with buyers to exclusive listings with buyers. This is the opportunity for you to professionalize the buyer's side of your real estate business. Won't it feel great being out of your subservient role with buyers? What will make it feel even better is that it will also be the opportunity for you to double your commissions by working with buyers in a professional manner.

CHAPTER 2

The Changing Real Estate Market

We are experiencing a changing real estate market as we write this and you read this. Today we are going from open listings with buyers to exclusive listings with buyers. This is the same process that occurred one hundred years ago in the progression from open listings with sellers to exclusive listings with sellers. This process with sellers took about twenty years.

The process with buyers has been a long time in coming. Several attempts have been made to introduce exclusive listings with buyers over the last 30 years. Just when the time seemed right for the real estate industry to implement exclusive listings with buyers in the normal market and buyer's market periods, however, a seller's market would arrive on the scene.

The problem has been the periods of annual double-digit price appreciation that have occurred in these seller's markets during this period. All progress with implementing exclusive listings with buyers was halted by the stampede to acquire inventory as the seller's markets took hold. We are going to share with you our experience in being involved in the real estate business over the last 30 years and how we developed our paradigm of working with buyers.

30-Year Time Line of Real Estate Markets, 1977–2006

| 1977–1979 | Seller's Market |
| 1980–1982 | Anti–Real Estate Market |

1983–1984	Buyer's Market
1985–1986	Normal Market
1987–1989	Seller's Market
1990–1992	Buyer's Market
1993–1999	Normal Market
2000–2001	Buyer's Market
2002–2006	Seller's Market

Our Experience

Bill entered the real estate business in Southern California in January 1977. He found himself at the beginning of the greatest seller's market that had yet occurred in real estate. As a salesman with the largest independent real estate company in the nation, Tarbell Realtors, Inc., Bill was trained to farm an area of 250 to 300 homes within a few miles of his company's real estate office. Bill's farming efforts quickly paid off. He began making money listing sellers in his farm area and having his listings sell.

Bill quickly became a top salesman in his company and was recognized as a million-dollar producer in 1978 and 1979. Bill pursued acquiring his broker's license as the seller's market continued. Bill then opened his own company, the Pisces Real Estate Company (you have to love that California connection) in January 1980. It was then that Bill discovered the cyclical nature of the real estate business.

Federal Reserve

Over the next 18 months, the Federal Reserve raised interest rates to the stratosphere to combat inflation. The real estate market practically ground to a halt. In many areas of the country, real estate prices not only stopped going up, they started going down! Bill, along with every other real estate broker, had many seller listings and few qualified buyers.

Instead of this meaning you were going to have automatic real estate success, quite the opposite was true. Having seller listings meant you were putting money into marketing and nothing was happening. None of your listings were selling because buyers could not qualify for a loan with interest rates as high as 17 percent.

The Anti–Real Estate Market, 1980–1982

Although we could call 1980, 1981, and 1982 a part of a buyer's market period in our 30-year time line, a more accurate designation would be to call these three years the anti–real estate market. The Federal Reserve was committed to stopping inflation, and to them that meant stopping the real estate market in its tracks.

Bill had to develop ways to help his sellers creatively finance the sale of their properties. Otherwise, there were going to be no sales. During this anti–real estate market, also known as a buyer's market, the idea of making an exclusive listing agreement with a buyer never entered anyone's mind. Survival was all Bill or anyone else in the real estate business could think about.

Buyer's Market, 1983–1984

Chantal entered the real estate business in the Dallas, Texas, metroplex in 1983. She found herself at the end of what we have called the anti–real estate market and the beginning of a buyer's market. As a salesperson with one of the largest Century 21 real estate companies in the nation, Chantal was trained to concentrate on getting exclusive seller listings. This is after three years of real estate companies going down the drain concentrating on seller listings. She received no training on how to work with buyers.

The old-timers in her office told Chantal how hard the real estate business had become. They lamented about the good old days of the late 1970s. Too bad she had not been in the real estate business then, they told her. Chantal took seller listings and then worked hard to bring in buyers to buy them. In her first six months in the business, she sold more than $1.5 million. She put the old-timers to shame.

Chantal realized that the quickest way to make money in the real estate business was to work with a buyer until they bought something. She saw that the future of real estate was in controlling the buyer. Even as a salesperson, Chantal would have the buyer sign a one-paragraph commitment agreement. Essentially, the buyer would commit to using Chantal if and when they bought something.

Normal Market, 1985–1986

After Chantal became a broker, we mentioned in the Preface that she began requiring buyers to deposit their earnest money into her broker's trust account before she would work with them. This was in 1985. We also mentioned in the Preface that Bill required buyers to provide a retainer of 0.5 percent of the upper limit of the projected purchase price before he would work with them. This was 1986.

Seller's Market, 1987–1989

The year 1987 marked the first seller's market in seven years. A major shakeout of the real estate industry had occurred during the 1980s up to this point. Many real estate businesses had failed. Many real estate licensees had gone into other lines of work.

Although we both continued to work the buyer's side of our real estate businesses using exclusive buyer listings in the seller's market of 1987 to 1989, the real estate industry as a whole was delighted to do business as usual. Happy days were here again for the exclusive seller-listings side of the business.

Buyer's Market, 1990–1992

We were both poised to take advantage of the buyer's market of 1990 to 1992. Chantal was writing eighty offers a week. Unfortunately, she encountered the entrenched seller-listing broker arrogance that existed at that time. The seller-listing brokers took it upon themselves to decide which of Chantal's buyer investor offers they would present to their sellers and which offers they would decide to reject on their own and not present to their sellers.

And you thought it was just doctors who played God! Once Chantal found out that her offers were not being presented but were being arbitrarily dismissed by the seller-listing brokers, the proverbial you know what hit the fan. After she filed a complaint with the Texas Real Estate Commission (TREC), more than forty brokers in the Dallas metroplex received warning letters from TREC threatening disciplinary action against them for violating their fiduciary duty to their sellers by not presenting all offers.

Meanwhile, Bill was developing and presenting courses on how to list buyers. These courses began in San Diego, California. It seemed like the time was right to create a groundswell of support for exclusive buyer listings. California was the largest real estate market in the country. California was also home to the largest number of real estate licensees in the country. Real estate market and industry trends start in California.

Normal Market, 1993–1999

In 1993, Bill was a director of the San Diego Association of Realtors. He was the chairman of the education committee of the San Diego Association. He was also a director of the California Association of Realtors. He also served on the education committee for the state association.

This seemed to be the time that Chantal in Texas and Bill and his partner, who was the San Diego Association president, in California were poised to make a significant impact on educating the real estate industry on the benefits of exclusive buyer listings. Traveling throughout the country in the early 1990s, we found rank-and-file agents everywhere receptive to exclusive buyer listings.

Unilateral Offer of Subagency

Organized real estate at the national level was not interested in exclusive buyer listings. And Texas was even worse! The problem was the entrenched Multiple Listing Service model that presented a unilateral offer of subagency from the seller-listing brokers to the brokers who brought the buyers.

What this means in English is the seller-listing brokers felt they were in control of the real estate industry. By making the brokers who brought them buyers their subagents, the seller-listing brokers could continue to control the real estate business. In other words, the seller-listing brokers thought they had nothing to gain by supporting the implementation of exclusive buyer listings.

We felt this thinking was flawed on the part of the seller-listing brokers. During the rest of this decade, there was not enough of a groundswell from the rank-and-file real estate agents to have the real estate profession professionalize its working with buyers. Everyone was too busy figuring out how to integrate this newfangled ever-changing computer technology into their real estate business.

Active Real Estate Investors

We were active real estate investors in this period. We decided not to renew our real estate broker's licenses in the mid-1990s. We did not want to have any fiduciary responsibility toward sellers with regard to any of our real estate investment deals.

We also began collaborating on writing real estate how-to books. In 1996, the second edition of *How to Sell Your Home Without a Broker* (Hoboken, NJ: Wiley) came out. When Bill wrote the first edition in 1990, he did it to have something to give to the many for sale by owners he was encountering as he was representing buyers exclusively.

Obviously, these for sale by owners did not want to pay a real estate commission. Yet they were for the most part clueless when it came to understanding anything that was involved in having a successful real estate transaction. Bill had to work both sides of the deal for half the commission.

The book showed the for sale by owners the complexity of trying to sell a home without the professional help of a real estate agent. As the syndicated columnist Robert Bruss said in his *Los Angeles Times* book review, "real estate agents have nothing to fear from this book." The book was designed to drive for sale by owners into the arms of an agent.

Buyer's Market, 2000–2001

The buyer's market of 2000 to 2001 came and went before we knew it. With the tech and stock market meltdowns and the terrorist atrocities of 9/11 dominating the period, the real estate industry was in a ho-hum state.

We had found our niche researching and writing how-to real estate investment books. We found very few real estate agents who would ask us if we wanted them to represent us as we made investment offers.

Seller's Market, 2002–2006

This seller's market will go down in history as the greatest seller's market of all time. Get seller listings. Get seller listings. Get seller listings. This was the battle cry of every real estate broker to their salespeople throughout the land.

We marveled at the resilient nature of the real estate industry. We continued to make real estate investments and write real estate books. Every once in a while, a real estate agent would ask us if we wanted them to represent us in a real estate buying transaction. We always declined because we wanted to represent ourselves.

Normal Market, 2007–2017

We feel we are on the verge of a protracted normal real estate market with localized dips into buyer's markets. Remember, we define a normal real estate market as striking a balance between sellers and buyers. It is neither a seller's market nor a buyer's market. This normal real estate market will last 8 to 12 years. Although a seller's market could break out at any time, we recommend you not hold your breath waiting for a seller's market to happen anytime soon.

This is actually good news for the real estate industry. This next 8- to 12-year period of a normal real estate market will provide a stable real estate market as a background for implementing exclusive buyer listings. Now is the time for you to do the work to implement exclusive buyer listings in your real estate business so you can be ahead of the competition.

Incentive

We want to give you some incentive for implementing buyer listings. The best incentive we can give you is a monetary incentive. We have already told you that you will double your commissions working with buyers after you implement exclusive buyer listings.

The other incentive we can give you is the education incentive. Knowledge is power. You, at the very least, are going to have to be able to talk intelligently with today's sophisticated real estate buyers. What are you going to do when a buyer asks you to represent them? The first thing we have to figure out is who pays real estate commissions.

Who Pays Real Estate Commissions?

If we asked you to tell us who pays the real estate commissions in a residential real estate transaction, 99 out of 100 real estate professionals would say that the seller pays real estate commissions. It seems so obvious that it almost looks stupid to even ask the question. However, let's do an experiment to see if we can get the real answer to this question.

The Experiment

If you were a real estate agent from another galaxy visiting our world, what would you observe about who pays real estate commissions? You would likely design an experiment that employs a strategy that we use here on our planet with regard to financial matters. Your strategy would be to follow the money.

Follow the Money

Let's look at a typical real estate transaction here on Earth. You are representing the seller in the sale of a four-bedroom, four-bathroom single-family home. The property is on the market for $495,000. As the listing agent, you have an exclusive authorization and right-to-sell agreement with the seller.

As part of the listing agreement, the seller agrees to pay you a 6 percent commission. If the property sells for the listed price, the seller will pay a $29,700 commission.

Real Estate Commission

Property Sales Price	$495,000
Percentage of Commission	× 6%
Commission Amount	$29,700

The Seller Has No Money

As part of your listing agreement, do you require the seller to place the $29,700 commission into your broker's trust account? Probably not, but a good idea! As part of your listing agreement, do you require the seller to place the $29,700 commission into the escrow that you are planning on using for the closing? Probably not, but again, a good idea!

Having the seller place the real estate commission into your broker's trust account or the closing escrow poses two problems. The first problem is convincing the seller to write a check for $29,700 to place in either your broker's trust account or the escrow. Although it may sound like an impossibility to convince the seller to write the check, we know some of you out there are more than capable of making that happen!

The second and more major problem is that most sellers do not have $29,700 sitting in their checking account! Although you may convince them to write the check and they would like to oblige you, there is no money for the seller to do so. The money the seller has to pay the real estate commission is hopefully part of the equity they have in the property.

The Seller Has Equity in the Property

If the seller can sell the property for $495,000 and they owe $375,000 on the mortgage(s), then they have a gross equity of $120,000.

Seller's Gross Equity

Property Sales Price	$495,000
Mortgage(s)	$-375,000
Seller's Gross Equity	$120,000

Out of the seller's gross equity, they will be able to pay the real estate commission and closing costs associated with the transaction. In this case, the real estate commission is about 25 percent of the seller's gross equity.

Percentage Commission of Gross Equity

Commission	$29,700
Gross Equity	$120,000
$29,700 / $120,000 = 25\%$	

So far, if you were a real estate agent from another galaxy, you still have not discovered where the money for the real estate commissions in our real estate world comes from. Your strategy to follow the money is sound.

Buyers Pay Real Estate Commissions

If you were the listing agent, what would you have to tell our intergalactic real estate agent now? You have signed a written agreement with the seller. The written agreement says the seller will pay your real estate commission. And the seller has no money to pay the real estate commission. How smart are you?

It is only when a buyer comes on the scene that the money shows up. Think about it. Let's say you find a buyer who makes an offer of $490,000 on your listing. Your seller accepts the buyer's offer. You are really getting excited. If this deal closes, you will make $29,400 in commission.

Real Estate Commission

Property Sales Price	$490,000
Percentage of Commission	× 6%
Commission Amount	$29,400

Let's say in the offer the buyer is making a 10 percent down payment of $49,000. The buyer is obtaining new financing for 90 percent of the purchase price or $441,000. The total of the buyer's down payment and the new buyer financing is the $490,000 purchase price.

Purchase Price

Buyer Down Payment	$49,000
New Buyer Financing	+$441,000
Purchase Price	$490,000

Once the buyer's down payment and new financing are processed in the closing, then the seller is credited with $490,000 on their side of the ledger. Now, after the seller's existing loan of $375,000 is paid off and their closing costs of $9,100 are subtracted, they have the money to pay your real estate commission.

Seller Money

Purchase Price	$490,000
Existing Loan	−$375,000
Closing Costs	−$9,100
Seller Money	$105,900

Real Estate Commission

Seller Money	$105,900
Commission Amount	−$29,400
Seller Net	$76,500

If you asked the intergalactic real estate agent where the money came from to pay your real estate commission, our visitor would unhesitatingly tell you. As a result of our visitor's experiment of following the money, it is obvious to them that the buyer paid your real estate commission.

The combination of the buyer's down payment and their ability to obtain new financing was the source of the funds for completing the real estate transaction, including the real estate commission. Is it obvious to you yet?

In the next chapter, we will look at the phenomenon of why buyers are lookie-loos. The old working-with-buyers paradigm keeps the real estate industry stuck with working with buyers for free.

And as we have just learned from our intergalactic visitor, buyers are the people with the money. Why would you work with the people who have the money and not have an exclusive agreement with them?

Why Buyers Are Liars, Flakes, and Lookie-Loos

We said in Chapter 1 that the real estate industry paradigm for buyers is that buyers come in one of three categories. Category 1 is that buyers are liars. Category 2 is that buyers are flakes. Category 3 is that buyers are lookie-loos. This paradigm dictates how buyers are going to occur for you.

In this chapter, we want to show you why buyers prove themselves to be liars, flakes, and lookie-loos. Remember lookie-loos are little cartoon characters that would just race through a seller's home with no intention of buying. Lookie-loos waste the seller's time, the seller's agent's time, and your time if you are working with them as your buyers.

It looks like from inside the real estate industry paradigm for buyers that you are being victimized by buyers. This paradigm for buyers gives you no power over or with your buyers. We want you to come to a revelation by the time you complete this chapter.

The Paradigm Is the Problem

As we said in Chapter 1, the bottom line is that the paradigm regarding buyers is completely shaped by your thinking that only sellers are worthy of your representation. The real estate industry interacts with buyers with an open-listing mentality.

However, we are not talking to the real estate industry in this chapter. We are talking to you. What are you going to do to double your commissions working with buyers? If you are going to wait for the real estate industry to come along and tell you it is okay to make money with buyers in the same way that you make money with sellers, you are going to have a long wait.

Give Us the How-To

We know some of you are already saying okay, we get it. We have to work with buyers in a more professional manner. Just get on with it and give us the how-to. We invite you to have patience. After all, the attempts at professionalizing the buyer's side of the real estate industry have been going on for twenty-plus years. We think now this is an idea whose time has come.

We are suggesting that you change the paradigm of how you work with buyers before you get into the how-to of the new paradigm. Otherwise, the new paradigm will be swallowed up by the old paradigm. The old paradigm is not going to go away without a fight. The rest of this book will teach you the how-to of implementing the new paradigm of working with buyers.

We also know some of you are still reserving judgment on whether you agree that the paradigm is the source of the problems you have working with buyers. You are still playing the blame game and making it the buyer's fault. That is the existing paradigm fighting to stay in control.

What Is a Paradigm?

We are going to assume you know nothing about paradigms. That way we can start at the beginning. We have been using this word *paradigm* for three chapters now. Perhaps before we can talk about changing paradigms we had better figure out what a paradigm is.

A paradigm is a way of thinking. Another way to say this is that a paradigm is a pattern of thinking. A paradigm shapes the information your brain can even detect. A way of thinking that is foreign to your way of thinking will automatically be regarded as strange, suspect, and ultimately dangerous. As we have said, the old paradigm will not give in to the new paradigm without a fight.

Paradigm Example 1

Five hundred years ago, a dominant paradigm of the day was that the earth was the center of the universe. It was obvious from commonsense observation that the sun, the moon, the planets, and the stars revolved around the earth. This astronomical paradigm was supported by the religious paradigm of the day in Europe.

The religious paradigm said God made the earth as the center of the universe and put the sun, the moon, the planets, and the stars around it. Man as God's most exalted creation was placed on the earth to be at the center of this universe. When scientists of the day such as Copernicus and Galileo proposed a new paradigm that the earth revolved around the sun, the old paradigm reacted with fearsome attacks.

Galileo was brought before the pope in Rome and told to recant his new paradigm or face excommunication from the Roman Catholic Church. There was also the additional matter that he would be killed after he was excommunicated if he did not recant. Excommunication assured that he would be going to hell after he was killed.

Galileo recanted and lived to see his new paradigm eventually vindicated by other scientists of the day. It was not until 1992, however, that the Roman Catholic Church confessed it was wrong in 1633 and removed the tarnish on Galileo's name from its official records.

Paradigm Example 2

We want you to experience one of your existing paradigms. We would like you to read the following passage out loud.

> Paris
> In The
> The Spring
> XOXOXO

What did you read out loud? Did you read out loud, "Paris in the spring"? What about the XOXOXO? Did you read out loud, "Paris in the spring XOXOXO"? Good for you. But that is not what it said. Or did you read out loud what it actually said, "Paris in the the spring XOXOXO"?

If you missed the second *the,* you didn't miss it because you don't know how to read. You missed the second *the* in "Paris in the the spring XOXOXO" because of your reading paradigm. According to your reading paradigm, the second *the* is not supposed to be there. So even though the second *the* is there, you do not see it. Even as we are writing this manuscript, the Microsoft Word program is underlining the second *the* in red, telling us it is not supposed to be there!

Our point is that paradigms are very powerful. Anything that is outside of the paradigm is rejected. Anything that does not fit the paradigm is regarded by the paradigm as nonexistent. Are you starting to get a sense that paradigms are pervasive? Are you realizing that paradigms can control not only your perception of reality but can actually shape reality?

Seeing the Real Estate Industry Paradigm

We have said that the current paradigm of the real estate industry requires that you work for free when you work with buyers. Or, at best, this paradigm requires that you work for many hours before you are compensated. We also said we know that in your paradigm of working with buyers you have many qualms about asking a buyer to agree to pay you a real estate commission.

Let's see how the paradigm of the real estate industry shapes your paradigm working with buyers. We want to get at the "Paris in the the spring XOXOXO" aspect of this paradigm. We want you to see that this paradigm has buyers occur for you as liars, flakes, and lookie-loos.

We also want you to see that you did not invent the real estate industry buyer's paradigm. You literally inherited this paradigm when you entered the real estate industry. The buyer's paradigm you inherited is as automatic as the seller's paradigm you inherited.

As part of how the paradigm works, it says that because you are the new kid on the block you are expected to accept the real estate industry the way you find it. And the paradigm tells you that if you are smart, you will learn the ropes and not rock the boat. We think it is time to rock the boat.

Real Estate Industry Paradigm in Action

The real estate industry paradigm tells you when you first get into the business that the only way to make money is to have seller listings. Remember this is the existing paradigm talking. Existing paradigms tend to be very narrow-minded and exclude anything that is outside the paradigm.

Although having seller listings is certainly a way to make money in the real estate business, it is not the only way to make money in the real estate business. There are at least nine other ways to make money in the real estate business with your real estate license. It is true you can make money without having a real estate license in several of these nine other ways. But you have your license, right?

Nine Other Ways to Make Money in the Real Estate Business

The nine other ways to make money in the real estate business include working with buyers, being a real estate lender, making real estate investments, being an appraiser, managing property, being a real estate consultant, teaching real estate, being a real estate expert witness, and writing about real estate topics. Obviously, our focus in this book is working with buyers.

Seller Listings

When we first got into the real estate business, we were told that by having seller listings we would make money because eventually the seller listings would sell. We were told that we didn't really need to spend time with buyers. Someone else would bring a buyer to buy our seller listings.

This struck us as rather odd. The question we had was who were these licensees who were going to bring the buyers? And having buyers sounded like a pretty good place to be. With a buyer, you would have a sale. If you had a sale, you were going to make money.

Bring Your Own Buyer

We were also told that if we brought a buyer to buy one of our seller listings, then we would get both sides of the transaction. This would double the amount of real estate commission we would make.

Let's say you were just the seller-listing agent on a property that sold for $300,000. If the seller agreed to pay a 6 percent commission and your office split the commission 50/50 with an outside broker that brought the buyer, 3 percent, or $9,000, would come to your office, and 3 percent, or $9,000, would go to the outside broker.

Your Office Commission

Sales Price	$300,000
Office Percentage	× 3%
Your Office Commission	$9,000

Outside Broker Commission

Sales Price	$300,000
Outside Broker Percentage	× 3%
Outside Broker Commission	$9,000

If your commission split with your broker was 50/50, then you would receive $4,500.

Your Commission

Your Office Commission	$9,000
Your Commission Split	× 50%
Your Commission	$4,500

If you brought the buyer for your seller listing, however, then your office would get the entire 6 percent commission. That would be $18,000.

Your Office Commission

Sales Price	$300,000
Office Percentage	× 6%
Your Office Commission	$18,000

This means that you would earn a commission for both sides of the transaction. You would be entitled to the same 50/50 office commission split. This would double the amount of real estate commission you would make having an outside broker bringing the buyer from $4,500 to $9,000.

Your Commission

Your Office Commission	$18,000
Your Commission Split	× 50%
Your Commission	$9,000

This was the good kind of buyer according to the industry paradigm. If you worked with a buyer and didn't have any seller listings, however, then you were going to wind up in buyer hell.

Working with Buyers Can Be Hell

The industry paradigm says if you are working with buyers who are not buying your seller listings, you are going to experience buyer hell. Buyer hell is you working with buyers without a safety net. The safety net the industry paradigm provides you is seller listings.

No matter what mistakes you make working with buyers, if you have seller listings, that safety net will break your fall. What fall are we talking about? We are talking about the fall of spending your time and money working with buyers with no guarantee of compensation.

We were told to avoid working with buyers until we had established our seller-listing business. The paradigm taught us a painful lesson when we went ahead and worked with buyers before we had secured multiple seller listings. These are the buyers that the industry says are liars, flakes, and lookie-loos.

Buyers Are Liars

Chantal had a nice young couple come into her office looking to buy their first home. This happened the first three weeks she was in the business. She sat down with the couple and asked them a series of questions to find out what they could afford and, more importantly, what kind of property they wanted to live in. Chantal felt the young couple was serious about buying property.

Over a six-week period, Chantal worked with these buyers and began narrowing down the choices from an initial 120 possibilities. The tough part was that the couple didn't really know what style of house they wanted. They were not interested in the three properties Chantal had listed during this time period.

The Perfect House

Finally, Chantal found them the perfect house. It turned out that it was contemporary styling. When the couple saw the house, they became very excited. They said it was the perfect property for them.

Chantal asked them if they would like to write an offer on the property. The couple said yes, they would like to write an offer on the property. However, they told Chantal they had another appointment and would like to get together with her later that afternoon.

Category 1

Needless to say, the young couple never kept the late afternoon appointment they had made with Chantal to write the offer. Chantal never saw the couple again. It turned out that the next appointment the couple had was with their uncle. This uncle happened to be in the real estate business. The uncle wrote and presented an offer for the couple on the perfect property that Chantal had spent six weeks finding for them.

This was a classic category 1 buyers are liars experience for Chantal. This is the category 1 section wherein buyers tell you that they are going to buy property from you and then they buy it from someone else. After this experience, Chantal went on a seller-listing binge.

Buyers Are Flakes

Early in Bill's real estate career, he encountered a buyer who presented himself as a real estate investor. This buyer came into Bill's real estate office on a Saturday morning when Bill was on the up desk. This was Bill's first walk-in. According to the real estate paradigm, this meant that this buyer was Bill's client. The buyer announced he was a real estate investor. He told Bill he was in the market to buy five to ten properties within the next 30 days. Bill sat down with the buyer and took down all the parameters the buyer said he was looking for.

The investor said he was buying the properties for rental income. He was going to make a 25 percent down payment so he would be able to have a positive cash flow. The investor told Bill that the agent who found the properties first would be the agent the investor would use for all future real estate deals. The buyer left the office after about thirty minutes. Bill was EX-CIT-ED!

The price range the investor was looking at was around $50,000. Bill did the calculations in his head. If the investor bought five properties, that would be a total of $250,000 worth of real estate.

If the investor bought 10 properties, that would be a total of $500,000 worth of real estate.

Value of Ten Properties

Single Property	$50,000
Number of Properties	× 10
Value of 10 Properties	$500,000

Bill quickly calculated the amount of commission he was going to make. He was on a 50/50 split with his company. At the minimum, if Bill found five properties that were listed with other brokers, he would make 1.5 percent of $250,000 or $3,750!

Minimum Commission for Bill

Value of Five Properties	$250,000
Bill's Percentage	× 1.5%
Bill's Commission	$3,750

At the maximum, if Bill found 10 properties that were listed with other brokers, he would make 1.5 percent of $500,000 or $7,500!

Maximum Commission for Bill

Value of 10 Properties	$500,000
Bill's Percentage	× 1.5%
Bill's Commission	$7,500

Within a week, Bill had shown the investor 15 properties. Each of these properties was in the $50,000 price range. Also, each of the properties met the investor's requirement of being three or four bedrooms and two bathrooms. Unfortunately for Bill, none of these properties were his seller listings.

After the investor said no to making an offer on the first 5 properties, Bill began to get a bad feeling. After the investor said no to making an offer on the first 10 properties, Bill began to suspect something was off with this buyer. After the investor said no to making an offer on all 15 properties, Bill asked the investor what was the problem?

Category 2

The buyer admitted to Bill that he did not have any money. He thought he would have $10,000 in about six months. The buyer said he was interested in being a real estate investor. He just thought it would take Bill a much longer time to find him properties that met his parameters. The buyer actually had the audacity to compliment Bill on how diligently he had worked in finding 15 properties so quickly.

This was a classic category 2 buyers are flakes experience for Bill. This is the category 2 section wherein buyers blow into your office, bragging that they are going to buy this property and that property and a third property. After this experience, Bill concentrated on getting seller listings.

Buyers Are Lookie-Loos

This is our favorite real estate industry buyer paradigm category. It so nails the industry paradigm for buyers. We have said that lookie-loos were a creation of a national real estate company. Little did they know they were creating the poster child for buyers being unrepresented by the real estate industry.

We said at the beginning of this chapter that by the time you got to the end of this chapter we wanted you to come to a revelation. The revelation we wanted you to come to is that buyers are liars, flakes, and lookie-loos because of your paradigm! More accurately said, we wanted you to see a distinction between the paradigm the real estate industry has working with buyers and your paradigm working with buyers.

Choice

You have a choice with regard to the business model you will operate from. You can continue to operate out of the real estate industry paradigm you inherited, or you can change it. You can continue to have buyers occur as liars, flakes, and lookie-loos. Sometimes you will make money, but more often you will not.

We encourage you to actively change the way you operate your real estate business and to represent buyers in a whole new way. In a way that will make you money working with buyers every time. The choice is yours.

So let's get on with designing this new business model: the representing buyers paradigm. In the next chapter, we will give you five answers to the question: Why list buyers? The answers are:

1. It is in the buyer's best interest.
2. It is in your best interest.
3. You are worth it.
4. You will be more professional.
5. To prevent divided agency.

CHAPTER 4

Why List Buyers?

T his chapter is about beginning to design the new paradigm for working with buyers. You must build a case for the validity of the new model step by step. Once you accumulate enough evidence for the new way of doing business, then you can feel comfortable operating from it.

Also, in this chapter we are going to give you five answers to the question, "Why list buyers?" These five answers are: (1) it is in the buyer's best interest, (2) it is in your best interest, (3) you are worth it, (4) to be a professional, and (5) to prevent divided agency.

The place we will start to answer the question "Why list buyers?" is with the simple adage, "What is good for the goose is good for the gander." This adage can be applied across many situations and relationships. Here we are using it in the context of working with real estate sellers and real estate buyers.

Why List Sellers?

Let's first ask the question, "Why list sellers?" This will help us get at answering the question, "Why list buyers?" Listing sellers is such a primary part of the real estate industry paradigm that it almost sounds ridiculous to ask the question. When we asked this question of 73 real estate professionals, many of them had this answer as their first response, "Are you kidding me? What a dumb question."

We told them we were serious and pressed them to really look and answer the question. We received the following answers.

Top 10 Answers to the Question, "Why List Sellers?"

10. My broker told me to list sellers.
9. This is the way I do business.
8. I always list sellers.
7. I can only spend my time with a seller who signs a listing.
6. I know the listing will eventually sell.
5. I have to have a seller listing before I can put the property on the MLS.
4. I would have to have a listing before advertising the property.
3. I do not work for free.
2. I want to know that if the property sells I will receive my commission.
1. I want exclusive control of the seller.

Let's get back to our adage. If the real estate industry says something is good when working with sellers, we think it is reasonable to use that same something and have it be good when working with buyers. Looking at our top 10 answers, the real estate industry says it is good to work with sellers in the following ways.

Good for the Goose, Good for the Gander

Paraphrasing some of our top 10 answers, we learned that it is good to work with sellers in a consistent manner. *This is the way to always do business.* It is good to have a high regard for your time. *My time is valuable.*

It is good to be guaranteed to make money in your business. *I am guaranteed to be paid for services rendered.* And finally, it is good to be in control. *I am in control of my business.*

New Paradigm

In designing your new paradigm of working with buyers, we think it would be good for you to work in a consistent manner with buyers just as you work with sellers. We think it would be good for you to have a high regard for your time working with buyers just as you do with sellers. We also think it would be good for you to be guaranteed to make money and be in control of your business working with buyers just as you do with sellers.

Why List Buyers?

Now it's time to present our top 5 answers to the question, "Why list buyers?" Because we are designing a new paradigm for working with buyers we are giving you the top 5 answers rather than the top 10 answers. Besides, if you pay close enough attention, by the time you have finished reading the rest of this chapter, you will be operating out of the new paradigm the next time you work with buyers.

1. It Is in the Buyer's Best Interest

"It is in the buyer's best interest" is the first answer to our question, "Why list buyers?" Again, if it is good for the goose, it is good for the gander. The real estate industry's business model of working with sellers settled once and for all that it is in the seller's best interest to be listed with one real estate agent. We say it is in the buyer's best interest to be listed with one real estate agent.

Let's look at it from the buyer's point of view. The buyer pulls out the real estate section of the paper. What is advertised are all the seller listings. The buyer circles the ads the buyer finds of interest. Then the buyer goes on the Internet or calls the seller-listing agents to find out more information on the properties. Ten to fifteen phone calls and e-mails later, the buyer may have eliminated all but three or four properties.

How much time and effort will it take for the buyer to make these ten to fifteen phone calls and e-mails? Perhaps it will take the buyer one to three hours. Then the buyer will be leaving messages and waiting for return calls and e-mails. The buyer will have to devise a system to keep track of all the different properties and the information about them.

How would it work for the buyer if the buyer had one real estate agent working for them? The buyer still might want to look at the real estate ads in the paper or go online. But then the buyer would call you as their exclusive buyer's agent to make all the phone calls and e-mails to check out the properties. How much time and effort does that save the buyer?

One Step Further

Let's take it one step further. As the buyer begins to think about buying real estate, a whole host of questions comes flooding into their mind. How much of a loan am I qualified for? Is my down payment big enough? Who should I use to do the closing? Do I need a real estate attorney? What about title insurance?

As the buyer's exclusive agent, you can provide them all the answers to their questions in a timely manner. The buyer makes one phone call to you, and you take care of the rest. The buyer does not have to rely on getting answers and information from multiple real estate agents in a hit-or-miss manner over a prolonged period of time.

Pause Button

We are hitting the pause button here to address what we know some of you are thinking. Some of you are thinking, "Chantal and Bill, this is how we already work with a buyer. We already have the buyer's best interest in mind. We don't need a new paradigm to do what we are already doing."

Congratulations, then you already have a leg up on implementing the new paradigm over agents who are not working with buyers the way you are. Remember, we are only one answer into answering our question, "Why *list buyers?*"

2. It Is in Your Best Interest

"It is in your best interest" is the second answer to our question, "Why list buyers?" We could give you many examples of situations in which this is true. Let's look at some of these situations to make our point.

Have You Ever Lost a Buyer to _____?

Let's pick up on our theme of have you ever lost a buyer to _____? In the Preface, we filled in the blank with four situations. These four situations were (1) an open house, (2) new home construction, (3) a for sale by owner, and (4) another real estate licensee.

An Open House

Chantal and Bill each have experienced the loss of a buyer to an open house. Bill was working with a buyer who wanted to live in a condominium. Bill showed the buyer a unit that the buyer did not like. Bill did not bother to show the buyer another unit that had the same floor plan in the same complex.

The company that had the listing on the other unit held that unit open on the Sunday after Bill had shown his buyer the similar unit. The buyer was looking at the complex without Bill and went into the open house. Even though the buyer had told Bill that she did not like the floor plan, you can guess what happened.

She was enthralled with the color of the paint and carpeting. She loved the decorator touches the owner had made in the unit. All of a sudden, she could see herself living there. When the agent holding the open house saw her excitement, the agent asked if she would like to make an offer.

The rest, as they say, is history. Bill called the buyer on Tuesday. She had just heard from the other agent. Her offer had been accepted. She was thrilled to share her wonderful news with Bill. She even invited him to come to her future house warming!

This story would have had a happy ending for Bill if he had a buyer listing. The buyer would have called Bill to write the offer on the second condo. Why would the buyer have called Bill if there was a buyer listing in place? Because the buyer would have to pay Bill a real estate commission regardless of who the real estate agent was who wrote the accepted offer!

New Home Construction

Chantal was working with buyers who wanted either a new home or a home that was less than three years old. The buyers told her this information at their initial meeting. In the old paradigm working with buyers, Chantal's option would have been to spend her time and effort to find the buyers an existing home that was listed before the buyers found a new home they liked or not make any money.

The buyers found a new home development they liked three weeks after Chantal began working with them. The buyers visited the model homes of one of the builders in the development. They were very much impressed with the quality, location, and amenities.

This story did have a happy ending. Chantal was operating with these clients out of the new paradigm of working with buyers. At their initial meeting, when Chantal discovered the buyers were interested in a new home, she made an agreement with the buyers that she would represent them in negotiations with the builder.

The buyers agreed to pay her a fee of $50 per hour for the time Chantal worked for them on a new home purchase. If Chantal negotiated with the builder and the builder agreed to pay her a commission, then the buyers would not have to pay Chantal's hourly fee.

The builder would not agree to pay Chantal a commission. However, Chantal negotiated $5,000 worth of upgrades for the buyers from the builder. By the time the transaction was completed, Chantal had 13 hours of her time involved. She had earned $650 in fees.

The buyers were so pleased with Chantal's work, the $5,000 worth of upgrades, and the smoothness of the transaction, they gave her a $350 bonus. Chantal made a total of $1,000 on this transaction.

Hourly Rate	$50
Chantal's Hours	× 13
Chantal's Fees	$650
Chantal's Bonus	+ $350
Chantal's Total	$1,000

The impressive part of this story is that Chantal made money working with buyers who bought a new home. Although $1,000 may not seem like a lot of money, it was $1,000 more than she would have made if she was working with these buyers in the old buyer's paradigm. And three years later, she had the seller listing on this property.

A For Sale by Owner
Bill was working with buyers who he felt were very sincere people. After meeting with the couple and showing them several properties, it seemed that everyone was comfortable with the progress being made. This is about as good as it gets in the old paradigm working with buyers. Bill was working without a safety net with these buyers. In other words, he did not have these buyers listed.

Four weeks into working with these buyers, Bill got a call. The buyers had found a property they loved. It was a for sale by owner. The buyers had asked the for sale by owner about bringing Bill into the negotiations. The for sale by owner told the buyers he was not going to pay a real estate commission.

The buyers told Bill that they were sorry, but they were going to go ahead and make an offer on the property without him. If the deal didn't go through, they would like to be able to come back and work with Bill again to find another property! It is fairly obvious to see that it would have been in Bill's best interest to have listed these buyers.

Another Real Estate Licensee
We have already given you an example in Chapter 3 about losing a sale to another real estate licensee. Remember the nice young couple Chantal had come into her office looking to buy their first home? We told you this happened the first

three weeks she was in the business. Chantal found them the perfect house.

Chantal never saw the couple again. It turns out the next appointment the couple had was with their uncle. This uncle happened to be in the real estate business. The uncle wrote and presented an offer for the couple on the perfect property that Chantal had spent six weeks finding for them.

We said this was a classic category 1 buyers are liars experience for Chantal. This is the category 1 section wherein buyers tell you that they are going to buy property from you and then they buy it from someone else. Of course, Chantal would not have had this horrible experience if she had listed these buyers. How many buyers have you lost to another real estate licensee operating out of the old working with buyers paradigm?

3. You Are Worth It

"You are worth it" is the third answer to our question, "Why list buyers?" How many of you would like to make at least $100,000 per year in your real estate business? If you work 40 hours per week at $50 per hour for 50 weeks, you will make $100,000.

Make $100,000 in a Year

Work	40 Hours per Week
Hourly	× $50 per Hour
Weekly	$2,000
50 Weeks	× 50
Annually	$100,000

We have said that we already know that every one of you reading this book has no qualms about asking a seller to sign an exclusive authorization and right-to-sell listing agreement. You also have no qualms about asking the seller to agree to pay you, let's say, a real estate commission of 6 percent of the selling price. You are paid this commission if anyone, including the seller, brings a buyer who buys the property.

With the average selling price of real estate in the United States approaching $300,000, the average real estate commission is $18,000.

6% Real Estate Commission

Average Selling Price	$300,000
Real Estate Commission Percentage	× 6%
Real Estate Commission	$18,000

We know in your paradigm of working with buyers that you have many qualms about asking a buyer to agree to pay you a real estate commission. If you are working with a buyer who is looking for the average price home of $300,000, there is $18,000 in real estate commissions on the table. In your paradigm of working with buyers, you have all the liability of working with sellers but with no guarantee of compensation.

But how many hours would you have to work at $50 per hour to make $18,000? You would have to work 360 hours to make $18,000!

Hours to Work

To Make $18,000
At $50 per Hour
$18,000 / $50 per Hour = 360 Hours.

Are you comprehending this? You do not work anywhere near 360 hours to sell a listing. Nine 40-hour weeks is 360 hours! If you sell this listing in 100 hours of work, do you feel guilty about earning an $18,000 commission?

You would be being paid $180 per hour for your services rendered.

Services Rendered

$18,000 Commission
100 Hours Worked
$18,000 / 100 Hours = $180 per Hour
(We are assuming you bring the buyer.)

Let's say you are only going to get the buyer's side of the commission, which would be 3 percent of $300,000, or $9,000.

3% Real Estate Commission

Average Selling Price	$300,000
Real Estate Commission Percentage	× 3%
Real Estate Commission	$9,000

If you work with a buyer for 100 hours, do you feel guilty about earning a $9,000 commission?

You would be being paid $90 per hour for your services rendered.

Services Rendered

$9,000 Commission
100 Hours Worked
$9,000 / 100 Hours = $90 per Hour

4. To Be a Professional

"To be a professional" is the fourth answer to our question, "Why list buyers?" How do you create being a professional working with buyers? You create being a professional working with buyers the same way you create being a professional working with sellers. You start by having a written agreement.

The written agreement you have between you and the seller is called an exclusive authorization and right to sell. We call this a seller's listing agreement. The written agreement you have between you and the buyer is called an exclusive authorization to locate property. It also can be called a buyer/broker agreement. We call it a buyer's listing agreement.

You complete the process of being a professional working with buyers the same way you complete the process of being a professional working with sellers. You establish an agency relationship with the buyer in the same way you would establish an agency relationship with the seller.

This agency relationship is in the buyer's best interest just as an agency relationship is in the seller's best interest. By establishing an agency relationship with the buyer, you become a fiduciary of the buyer. As a fiduciary of the buyer, you owe the buyer the highest care and consideration in all your actions. You must do what is in the buyer's best interest at all times.

5. To Prevent Divided Agency

"To prevent divided agency" is the fifth answer to our question, "Why list buyers?" Divided agency is bad. Divided agency occurs when by your words or actions you appear to be serving more than one real estate client in the same transaction as their fiduciary without their knowledge and consent.

Legally, you cannot be a fiduciary of the seller and a fiduciary of the buyer in the same transaction. The penalties that may be imposed if you are found to have engaged in a divided agency transaction include disgorgement of your real estate commission and loss of your real estate license.

Old Working with Buyers Paradigm

The old working with buyers paradigm can get you into trouble with divided agency. Any buyers you work with may think you are their agent from a fiduciary standpoint. If you sell them any multiple-listed properties, you are automatically a subagent of the seller. This means you may have a divided-agency relationship hazard with your buyers.

We will have an in-depth discussion of how the new way of working with buyers eliminates the pitfall of divided agency in Chapter 11. Suffice it to say here that having a buyer-listing agreement automatically makes you an agent of the buyer.

Where We Are

We said this chapter is about beginning to design the new paradigm for working with buyers. We said you have to build a case for the validity of the new paradigm step-by-step. We did this by giving our top five answers to the question, "Why list buyers?"

1. It is in the buyer's best interest.
2. It is in your best interest.
3. You are worth it.
4. To be more professional.
5. To prevent divided agency.

We also said that once you accumulate enough evidence for the new paradigm, then you can feel comfortable operating from it. In the next chapter, we will look at why buyers will list with you. Buyers are ready for the new paradigm. Buyers, like sellers, want to be represented in a real estate transaction. As an industry, our job is to give the buyers, as we do the sellers, what they want.

CHAPTER 5

Why Buyers Will List with You

This chapter is about interacting with real estate buyers. You will discover over the course of reading this chapter that buyers are ready, willing, and able to list with you. You will find that buyers are more than willing to meet you halfway in implementing the new working with real estate buyer's paradigm.

We live in the age of the consumer. The consumer is king and queen. A real estate purchase is the biggest ticket item that a consumer makes. Buyers in a real estate transaction want to know they are getting value for their money. The way for a real estate buyer to get the best value for their money is for you to represent them.

Consumers Are Demanding Value for Their Money

From the very rich to the rest of us, we, as consumers, demand value for our money. We all work too hard to get our money not to want to make it go as far as possible. With even the smallest purchase, we want to make sure we have shopped around and got the best possible price. A real estate purchase is no different. There just may be many more zeros on the price tag of the real estate than we are normally used to spending in a day.

You Get What You Pay For

The cheapest price does not mean you get the best value. The old expression *penny-wise and pound-foolish* certainly applies in today's world. Why would it make sense if when someone is making their most expensive consumer purchase as a real estate buyer, the real estate agents who are supposedly assisting them are doing so for free?

In other words, what is the catch? The catch is in the old working with real estate buyer's paradigm. Real estate buyers are paying real estate commissions through their down payments and ability to qualify for new financing. (See the discussion in Chapter 2 on who pays real estate commissions.) What is worse is that real estate buyers are not being represented by their real estate agents even though real estate buyers are paying their real estate agent's commission!

No Catch

In the new working with real estate buyer's paradigm, there is no catch. When a buyer signs a buyer-listing agreement with you, it is clear that you are being paid by them. It is also clear that you are representing them. And your job is to get them the property they want at the price and terms that they want.

Price and Terms

Why buyers will list with you is because they want to buy real estate for the best possible price and under the best possible terms. Having you represent them exclusively in a real estate transaction is the way to guarantee they will get value for their money. Buyers will get value for the money they are spending for the real estate and buyers will get value for the money they are paying you.

Example 1

After Bill first started listing buyers, the third buyer he listed benefited immediately from the new paradigm. In the old business model, a real estate agent could sometimes be put in the position of what we call shoehorning the buyer into a property. Bill did not have to shoehorn this buyer.

Shoehorning

Shoehorning occurs when the property does not quite fit the buyer and the buyer does not quite fit the property. The old way puts pressure on the agent to find something immediately and have the buyer write an offer or else lose the buyer to an open house, new construction, for sale by owner, or another licensee.

The real estate agent then may have to squeeze the buyer into a property to make a sale and receive a commission. It may work out to be a good property for the buyer. However, many times the buyer winds up with buyer's remorse and is not happy with the property or their real estate agent.

And because the real estate agent shoehorned the buyer into the property, buyer's remorse will not stop the deal from going through. However, the buyer will never use that real estate agent again either as a seller or as a buyer.

Buyer's Remorse

Buyer's remorse! Every buyer experiences the onset of the disease once their offer is accepted by the seller. Even real estate investors experience buyer's remorse. There is no known antidote or medication. The disease just has to run its course. For some buyers the disease is mild. For other buyers the disease is severe.

The buyers start having doubts about the purchase. Are they doing the right thing? Should they look at more properties? Did they offer too much? Can they really afford the monthly payments? Is the house big enough? Is the house too big?

What if they don't qualify for a loan? What if they *do* qualify for a loan? Sometimes buyer's remorse can become terminal. Then the buyer backs out of the deal. The deal is killed by buyer's remorse.

The Deal

Bill found a property for his buyer. The buyer wanted to make an offer. After writing the offer, Bill called the seller's listing agent to schedule an appointment to present an offer. The seller's listing agent informed Bill that another offer was coming in on the property. Bill was welcome to present his offer, but the seller would reserve the right to wait and hear both offers before making a decision.

Bill called his buyers and let them know what was going on. His buyers were very interested in the property but did not want to overpay. They told Bill to present their offer as written. They did not want to rewrite the offer and increase the price just because there was another offer. The property was listed for $202,000.

Bill presented his buyer's offer. The seller waited to hear the second offer and then countered both offers with the same sales price. The seller countered $200,000. Bill's buyer's offer was for $187,500.

Multiple Listed Property

Property Listed For	$202,000
Bill's Buyer's Offer	$187,500
Seller's Counteroffer	$200,000

Bill's buyers instructed Bill not to respond to the seller's counteroffer. The competing buyer accepted the seller's $200,000 counteroffer and bought the property.

Old Paradigm

In the old working with buyers paradigm, Bill would have felt the pressure of trying to shoehorn his buyers into this property. His buyers might have made a higher offer than the competing buyer and got the property. Bill would have made the sale and received a commission. But would Bill's buyers have got value for their money?

New Paradigm

In the new working with buyers paradigm, neither the agent nor the buyer feels any pressure to make a buy. The buyer does not have to buy the first or second property that you find for them. The buyer does not have to get into a bidding war with another buyer for the same property.

In the new paradigm, you will find the buyer the right property. In the new paradigm, you will negotiate the price and terms the buyer wants. In the new paradigm, the buyer will get value for their money in their real estate purchase. The buyer also will get value for the money they are paying you, and you will be guaranteed compensation for services rendered.

Example 2

So what happened to Bill's buyer who decided against pursuing the property in example 1? Bill went back to work and found them another property. This property was a for sale by owner. It was a comparable property to the property in example 1. However, it was on the market for $190,000.

Bill suggested writing an offer for $180,000. The buyers agreed and went ahead and wrote the offer. Bill called the for-sale-by-owner seller and told them he would like to present an offer. The seller agreed to an appointment to meet with Bill.

For-Sale-by-Owner Property

Asking Price	$190,000
Bill's Buyer's Offer	$180,000

For Sale by Owner Will Not Pay a Real Estate Commission

The first thing the for-sale-by-owner seller told Bill when Bill arrived for the appointment was that he would not pay Bill a real estate commission. Bill told the for-sale-by-owner seller that was not a problem. Bill's buyer was going to pay his real estate commission!

Bill presented the offer for $180,000. He told the seller that the buyer liked the seller's property but would not pay more than $180,000. The seller asked Bill if it would be worthwhile for the seller to counteroffer $185,000.

Seller's Proposed Counteroffer

Asking Price	$190,000
Bill's Buyer's Offer	$180,000
Seller's Counteroffer	$185,000

Bill told the seller that would be a waste of time. His buyer would not accept the seller's counteroffer of $185,000. The buyer would just have Bill find another property.

For-Sale-by-Owner Seller Accepts Offer

The for-sale-by-owner seller accepted Bill's buyer's offer of $180,000. Bill's buyer had agreed to pay Bill a 3 percent commission on the purchase price. This was $5,400.

Bill's Commission

Purchase Price	$180,000
Commission Percentage	$\times$ 3%
Bill's Commission	$5,400

Bill's buyer was very pleased with buying the property for $180,000. The buyer was even more pleased that even with paying Bill's real estate commission of $5,400, the buyer was effectively paying only $185,400 for the property.

Effective Purchase Price

Purchase Price	$180,000
Bill's Commission	+ $5,400
Effective Price	$185,400

This was less money than what the buyer had offered on the first property of $187,000 in example 1. By using Bill as a buyer's broker, the buyer got great value for their money in their real estate purchase. The buyer also got great value for the money they paid Bill.

Buyer Ahead

The buyer got $10,000 off the for sale by owner's asking price of $190,000 by paying only $180,000. The $5,400 in real estate commission the buyer paid Bill still left them $4,600 ahead of paying the for-sale-by-owner seller $190,000 for the property.

Buyer Ahead

Asking Price	$190,000
Effective Price	− $185,400
Buyer Ahead	$4,600

Bill's Added Benefit

The for-sale-by-owner seller was so impressed with the way Bill represented his buyer in the transaction, he asked Bill to represent him in buying his next property! The for-sale-by-owner seller recognized that Bill's buyer got value for their money in their real estate purchase. He wanted Bill to help him get the same value in his next real estate purchase.

Bill found a property that was on the market for $240,000. Bill's buyer offered $220,000. The seller counter-offered $230,000.

Property on the Market

Asking Price	$240,000
Bill's Buyer's Offer	$220,000
Seller's Counteroffer	$230,000

Bill got the seller to accept a counteroffer to the seller's counteroffer of $224,000. Bill saved his buyer $16,000 off the asking price.

Buyer Savings

Asking Price	$240,000
Counter to the Counter	− $224,000
Buyer Savings	$16,000

Bill's buyer had agreed to pay Bill a 3 percent commission on the purchase price. Remember, the final agreed upon purchase price was $224,000. The commission to Bill was $6,720. This seller was also a for sale by owner.

Bill's Commission

Purchase Price	$224,000
Commission Percentage	× 3%
Bill's Commission	$6,720

Again, Bill's buyer was very pleased with buying the property for $224,000. The buyer was even more pleased that even with paying Bill's real estate commission of $6,720 the buyer was effectively paying only $230,720 for the property.

Effective Purchase Price

Purchase Price	$224,000
Bill's Commission	+ $6,720
Effective Price	$230,720

Again, by using Bill as a buyer's broker, the buyer got great value for their money in their real estate purchase. The buyer also got great value for the money they paid Bill.

Buyer Ahead

The buyer got $16,000 off the for sale by owner's asking price of $240,000 by paying only $220,000. The $6,720 in real estate commission the buyer paid Bill still left them $9,280 ahead of paying the for-sale-by-owner seller $240,000 for the property.

Buyer Ahead

Asking Price	$240,000
Effective Price	− $230,720
Buyer Ahead	$9,280

Bill's Commissions

Bill had now made a total of $12,120 in real estate commissions with these two transactions in the new working with buyers paradigm.

Bill's Total Commissions

Commission from First Buyer	$5,400
Commission from Second Buyer	+ $6,720
Total Commissions	$12,120

In the old working with buyers paradigm, Bill would have made zero real estate commission dollars. That is because both of his buyers bought properties from for-sale-by-owner sellers! Only by having these buyers listed did Bill guarantee being compensated for the services he rendered.

Three Observations

We are going to conclude this chapter about why buyers will list with you with three observations on our part. Our first observation is if there are no real estate buyers there is no real estate market. Our second observation is a represented buyer is ready, willing, and able to buy. Our third observation is a represented buyer is a happy buyer.

No Real Estate Buyers = No Real Estate Market

The real estate industry is the last bastion of anticonsumer sentiment in big business today. Every major category of business that you can think of values their customers like gold. The customer who keeps coming back, the repeat customer, is the lifeblood of every successful company you can name.

We are constantly amazed that buyers have demonstrated such customer loyalty to the real estate industry. You would think that because of the old working with buyers paradigm, real estate buyers would have turned to attorneys or even insurance professionals to represent them in their real estate transactions. So far, they have not done so. Buyers have remained loyal to us.

Real Estate Buyers Want to Buy Real Estate

Real estate buyers want to buy real estate. Real estate buyers want to buy real estate from real estate agents. For those of you in business in between 1980 and 1982, in what we have called the anti–real estate market, you know from firsthand experience that when there were no buyers there was no real estate market.

You could have all the seller listings you wanted. It did not make a real estate market. Only when real estate buyers came back into the game did the real estate market recover. Today, let's treat real estate buyers like the gold that they are.

A Represented Buyer Is Ready, Willing, and Able to Buy

When we first got into the real estate business, we were both told that a true buyer was a buyer who was ready, willing, and able to buy real estate. A buyer was ready if the timing was right in their world to buy real estate. A buyer was willing if the buyer was committed to making a real estate purchase. A buyer was able if the buyer had the financial resources to make a real estate deal happen.

New Working with Buyers Paradigm

In the new working with buyers paradigm, we say a represented buyer is ready, willing, and able to buy real estate. Today's buyers want to be represented by you. Once they sign a buyer's listing agreement, today's real estate buyer brings the timing, commitment, and financial resources to make a real estate deal happen.

A Represented Buyer Is a Happy Buyer

Finally, a represented buyer is a happy buyer. A represented buyer gets what they want. The represented buyer gets the property they want. The represented buyer gets the price and terms they want.

And because a represented buyer is a happy buyer, you will get many enthusiastic referrals. Not to mention, the represented happy buyer being your lifelong real estate client whether they are buying or selling.

In the next chapter, we will show you how to make a listing presentation to buyers. You must make a listing presentation to buyers before you ask them to sign an exclusive buyer's listing agreement with you. The purpose of the presentation is for you to demonstrate expertise.

CHAPTER 6

Making the Listing Presentation to Buyers

In this chapter, we will show you how to make a listing presentation to buyers. You must make a listing presentation to buyers before you ask them to sign an exclusive buyer's listing agreement with you. You do not go into a seller's home and just start filling out the seller listing paperwork. So you certainly would not do that with a buyer either.

Just as you must demonstrate expertise and make a listing presentation to a seller before the seller will sign a seller's listing agreement, you must demonstrate expertise to a buyer before the buyer will sign a buyer's listing agreement. The same things apply to the buyer's listing presentation as to the seller's listing presentation.

You have to set a buyer listing appointment. Then you have to prepare for the appointment. At the appointment, you have to handle the logistics. What are you going to say at the appointment? How do you ask for a commitment from the buyer? What buyer listing agreement are you going to use? How long a listing period are you going to ask for?

Setting the Buyer's Listing Appointment

There are two main points to handle in the setting of the buyer's listing appointment. The first point to handle is when you are meeting with the buyer. The second point to handle is where you are meeting with the buyer.

When to Meet with the Buyer

We recommend you meet with the buyer in the evening. The best time we have found is after dinner. That way, you can have the buyer's undivided attention. The prime time to schedule the buyer's listing appointment is 7 P.M. This is of course if they work during the day.

Meeting during the day seems to invite interruption. You are going to be interrupted by the buyer's family and business day unfolding. You are going to be interrupted by your day unfolding.

We have found that meeting during a weekend day is also fraught with interruptions. Although it would seem that the buyer would have more uninterrupted time available to meet with you, we have found that this is not the case.

Weekends seem to be consumed by honey-do lists, family obligations, relaxing, catching up on needed sleep, and putting off making big decisions. You know, like the decision to sign a buyer's listing agreement with you!

Amount of Time for the Appointment

You will need a minimum of an hour and a half. We recommend you plan for two hours. So when you are talking to the buyer, let them know that you will be there at 7 P.M. and be out the door by 9 P.M.

Remember, no matter how brilliant you are, people today have the ability to pay attention for no more than 90 to 120 minutes. That is the length of most full-length feature movies.

You want to be professional with the buyer in setting the buyer's listing appointment. By specifying the 7 P.M. to 9 P.M. time line, you come across to the buyer as being a professional who is concerned with and considerate of the buyer's time.

Where to Meet with the Buyer

The best place to meet with the buyer is at the buyer's home. We like meeting with the buyer at the buyer's home so we can see what kind of property the buyer lives in. We also want to see the condition of the property. This way, we can know what expectations the buyer is bringing to the search for their next property.

The next best place to meet is at your real estate office. This provides a business and professional environment for the meeting. Meeting at your office works well with investor buyers. Although we will meet with a home buyer at our office, we prefer meeting with them at the buyer's home.

Where Not to Meet with the Buyer

Do not meet with the buyer at a restaurant or coffee shop. We say this for two reasons. The underlying message you convey when meeting at a restaurant or coffee shop is it is a social meeting. Let's get a bite to eat or let's get a cup of coffee so we can talk does not create a business context.

Do not meet with the buyer for the first time at a property the buyer is interested in seeing. You will wind up being trapped by the old working with buyers paradigm.

Almost Nothing Good Will Happen

One of five outcomes will occur from having an initial meeting with the buyer at a property. In all five outcomes, the buyer will think you are operating out of the traditional business model. And *you will be creating the buyer* in the image of the old paradigm.

The first outcome is the buyer calls you to show them a property, and you do. You come at the buyer's beck and call. The best outcome for you and the buyer is, by some miracle, the buyer allows you write an offer on the property that is accepted by the seller. This has never happened for us. Has it happened for you?

The second outcome is you show the buyer the property. The buyer then has the listing agent, one of the many agents who have already shown them property, or the buyer's aunt or uncle real estate agent writes an offer on the property that is accepted by the seller.

This is obviously bad for you. At first glance, it may look good for the buyer. However, just because a seller has accepted the buyer's offer written by a real estate agent who does not represent the buyer does not mean the buyer got a good deal. The buyer more than likely paid too much for the property.

The third outcome is you show the buyer the property. The buyer does not make an offer on the property. You never hear from the buyer again. This is bad for you and the buyer. You wasted your time once again working with a buyer in the old paradigm. The buyer missed out on working with you.

The fourth outcome is you show the buyer the property. The buyer is not interested in the property. But the buyer likes you and wants you to show them more property. Now it is too late to effectively present yourself as a professional and ask for a buyer's listing agreement. You have placed yourself in a subservient position to the buyer.

The fifth outcome is you arrive to show the buyer the property. The buyer stands you up and never arrives for the appointment. One more time, you have created a buyer in the image of the old paradigm. Take your pick. Is this buyer a liar, flake, or lookie-loo?

At the Buyer's Place of Business

Do not meet with the buyer at the buyer's place of business. Again, we say this for two reasons. The buyer will likely be interrupted by the demands of their business day. You will not have their undivided attention. And the buyer also will be in control of the meeting. This is not something you can allow.

Preparing for the Appointment

Once you have made an appointment with the buyer, you need to prepare for the appointment. The new working with buyers paradigm requires that you interact with a buyer in a professional manner.

You would not dream of going to a seller's listing presentation and just winging it. Each one of you has a set presentation you do when you are sitting at the seller's kitchen table. You prepare thoroughly for the appointment.

You know there are tens of thousands of dollars of real estate commissions on that seller's kitchen table. You may be competing for that seller listing with several other real estate agents. That does not faze you one bit. You know you will get the seller listing.

You must go into the buyer listing presentation with the same mind-set. There are tens of thousands of dollars of real estate commissions on the buyer's kitchen table. You know you will get the buyer listing. You are worth the money.

What to Bring to the Appointment

Here are the top five items to bring to the buyer's listing appointment. Some of you may have a top 7 or even a top 10. Once you have the top five handled, bring whatever else you think you will need.

What to Bring

1. A real estate professional.
2. Buyer-listing presentation notebook.
3. Buyer listing agreements.
4. Laptop computer.
5. Your calendar.

1. A Real Estate Professional

The first thing to bring to the buyer's listing appointment is you being a real estate professional. This means that you are operating out of the new paradigm.

It may take you a few buyer listing presentations before you feel completely at ease and comfortable. Relax. It took you a few seller-listing presentations before you felt completely at ease and comfortable. You want to make the buyer feel you have worked with other buyers in the new paradigm and it has worked out well for those buyers.

2. Buyer-Listing Presentation Notebook

The second thing to bring to the buyer's listing appointment is a personalized buyer-listing presentation notebook. The notebook should include the types of property that you can find for the buyer.

Types of Property You Can Find the Buyer
This would include the property that is seller-listed with your company and property-seller-listed by other brokers. It would also include for-sale by-owner property and new housing developments. Finally, you should mention that you will be able to find the buyer the perfect property once you know in writing what kind of property they want, even if that property is not on the market!

Company Policy
The notebook also should include a section that says your company policy is to exclusively represent buyers in a real estate transaction. It should then state as a fact that the real estate buyer pays real estate commissions because the real estate buyer is the party in the transaction with the money.

Letters of Recommendation
It is imperative for your success that you include letters of recommendation from former clients that you can show to the prospective buyer. In the beginning, you may have to include letters of recommendation from sellers. You may have to include letters of recommendation from buyers you worked with in the old paradigm.

The point is the more letters of recommendation you have the better. The prospective buyer will not read all of them. The prospective buyer may not even read one of them. However, the prospective buyer wants to see that you have letters of recommendation so that they feel comfortable that you can do a great job for them.

Your Credentials

Include a section on your credentials. This would include your real estate license designations (sale's or broker's). How long you have been in the real estate business. Professional real estate designations beyond your real estate license (GRI, CRS, MAI).

Educational degree(s) you hold (B.A., B.S., M.A., M.S., or Ph.D.). Also include other credentials, designations, and expertise you have. This could be things like securities and insurance licenses, local association or state committees, directorships, or offices you hold or have held.

For example, Bill's credential section would look like this:

Bill's Credentials

Licensed California real estate broker (1979).

Owner/broker the Pisces Real Estate Company (1980).

Co-owner/broker Real Estate Buyers Service (1986).

Founding member of the California Association of Buyer's Agents and the Institute for Real Estate Education (1991).

Director and chairman of the Education Committee of the San Diego Association of Realtors (1993).

Director and member of the Education and Taxation Committees of the California Association of Realtors (1993).

Licensed in securities (6 and 63) and insurance (life).

Certified tax preparer for the state of California.

Expert witness for buyers in real estate civil litigation.

Real estate instructor Anthony Real Estate Schools. College level and continuing education classes in real estate finance, economics, appraisal, property management, and taxation (1982–1991).

Real estate trainer, Bob Allen's Wealth Training (1990–1993).

3. Buyer Listing Agreements

The third thing to bring to the buyer's listing appointment is buyer listing agreements. Some areas have state-mandated forms that must be used by real estate licensees. Some areas have no state-mandated forms.

In Texas, for example, the Texas Real Estate Commission (TREC) mandates that all Texas real estate licensees must use TREC-approved and created forms in their real estate transactions. However, TREC does not produce a seller or buyer listing agreement. That is left to the real estate industry itself to produce.

In California, on the other hand, the California Association of Realtors provides real estate forms to its membership. However, the state of California does not mandate that its real estate licensees must use state-approved real estate forms.

Types of Buyer Listing Agreements

The California Association of Realtors produces at least five types of buyer listing agreements. These include a buyer broker agreement—exclusive, a buyer broker agreement—nonexclusive, a buyer broker agreement—nonexclusive/not for compensation, a buyer nonagency agreement, and a disclosure/consent for representing more than one buyer!

This is not to mention disclosure regarding real estate agency, confirmation of real estate agency relationship, commission agreement, single-party compensation agreement, termination of buyer agency, and the ready pack for buyer's agent. And you thought buyer listings were brand new!

Finding the Right Buyer Listing Agreement

Your job is to find the buyer listing agreement that works for you. First, check your company policy with regard to what buyer listing agreement your company wants you to use. If you are the broker and want to find a buyer listing form, check first with your local association of realtors, then your state association or your state licensing department.

4. Laptop Computer

The fourth thing to bring to the buyer's listing appointment is your laptop computer. You may never even open the laptop to do anything for your buyer's listing presentation. If you do not have a laptop, get one for your buyer listing presentations!

The fact that the buyer sees you with a laptop conveys to the buyer that you are a professional with up-to-date professional tools. This sends the buyer a powerful message that you have invested in your business and can get the job done for the buyer.

Some of you are proficient with the technology and may develop a PowerPoint buyer's listing presentation you will use at the buyer's listing appointment. Good for you. Just remember that some people may find it extremely uncomfortable looking over your shoulder or across the kitchen table to see your computer screen.

PowerPoint Pointers

For those of you who develop a PowerPoint buyer's listing presentation, we want to share with you our PowerPoint pointers. The content is pretty much up to you. We do not recommend you ever have the buyer listing agreement on the screen. That will be the fastest way to put the clients to sleep.

Remember, a picture is worth a thousand words. The simpler the information is on the screen the better. Never have a picture and then have writing at the bottom of the picture. The picture is already a thousand words. The writing takes away from the emotional impact of the picture. The picture will take away from the impact of the writing.

In making a PowerPoint presentation, you must always say the exact words on the screen. People will believe the words written on the screen over the words they hear coming out of your mouth. In fact people will begin to distrust the words coming out of your mouth if they consistently fail to match the words on the screen!

5. *Your Calendar*

The fifth thing to bring to the buyer's listing appointment is your calendar. Although this may seem obvious, it is quite important. Some of you may keep your calendar on your technology like a PDA, Blackberry, or laptop. That is fine with us.

However, we recommend you bring a paper calendar that is at least 12 inches square. We have found that it is much easier for the buyer to relate to the hard-copy calendar that they can see.

Purpose

The purpose for bringing your calendar is to match the buyer's calendar to your calendar to schedule times for you to show the buyer property. Also, you want to note any important dates on the buyer's calendar so as to avoid any scheduling conflicts or misunderstandings. Also, we use the calendar to make trial closes.

Trial Closes

Mr. Buyer, if we decide to do business, do you have your calendar handy? I would like to find out your availability to look at property this week.

Ms. Buyer, do you have your calendar handy? I would like to find a convenient time for you to speak to a loan representative. That way, we can get you prequalified for the best home you can afford.

Mr. and Mrs. Buyer, I will have time on Tuesday to find the perfect property for you. Would you be available to see it on Wednesday afternoon or Thursday afternoon?

At the Appointment

After you arrive at the buyer's home, you want to take control of the appointment immediately. Ask the buyer if you can sit at the kitchen table. Sit with your back to an outside wall. You want the buyer(s) to have their full attention on you and not be able to look beyond you to see what is happening in the rest of the house.

Request any distractions to the meeting be removed. You want televisions, music, or loud noises turned off or eliminated.

Pets and children need to be accommodated. However, you can politely ask for privacy while you are making your buyer listing presentation.

What to Say at the Appointment

Once you have handled the logistics of the meeting, it is time to get started. You first want to make sure you are on the same page with the buyer. We recommend you find something to talk about that is interesting to the buyer.

After a little conversation while sitting at the kitchen table, ask the buyer if it would be okay with them to take you on a tour of their home. That way, you can better understand what kind of space they are currently living in so you can find the perfect floor plan for them to move to.

Why Meeting at a Prospective Buyer's Home Is Important

Meeting at a prospective client's home serves two purposes. The first purpose is for you to really see how the buyer is living, how they are using their floor plan, and what needs to be changed in the property you find them to improve their quality of life.

After all, people usually do not think about moving unless the home they are living in is not working for them. The current house is too big or too small or too something that by moving can be alleviated.

The second and perhaps more important purpose is for you to get on the same page as the buyer. This may be the first time that you have met the buyer in person. By taking the home tour and finding something complimentary to say, you give the buyer time to warm up to you.

You have overcome the first hurdle with the buyer by being invited into their home for the buyer listing appointment. Now you are giving them the opportunity to size you up as someone they want to do business with. After all, the buyer will be trusting you to help them find their next home.

Back at the Kitchen Table

The home tour may have taken ten to fifteen minutes. After completing the home tour, return to the kitchen table. The buyer will have had time to feel comfortable about you being in their home. Now is the time to begin your buyer listing presentation. This is what you say:

Ms. Buyer, thank you so much for showing me your home. I would like to take a few minutes and show you how I propose we work together to find your next home. Would that be all right with you?

You always want to get permission from the buyer to take the next step in the buyer listing presentation. If for whatever reason the buyer is uncomfortable with proceeding, you must stop the presentation and find out what is going on.

What Is Going On?

Chantal reached this point in a buyer listing presentation and realized the buyer seemed a little nervous. When Chantal asked the buyer the question, **Would that be all right with you?,** the buyer confessed that she just remembered she had promised to return a phone call to her mother.

Chantal suggested the buyer give her mother a quick call and ask if it would be okay for her to call back after the appointment. The buyer made the quick call to mom and arranged to call back later. This took two minutes.

Without Chantal asking the question to get permission to proceed, the buyer would have been thinking about the unmade phone call to mom. She would not have been able to give her undivided attention to Chantal and Chantal's presentation. More than likely, Chantal would not have got the listing.

Agency Disclosure

Next, we recommend you spend some time on agency disclosure. We feel agency disclosure is the most important step in the buyer listing presentation. We say it this way: Agency disclosure opens the door to listing buyers. Remember, you are

in the education business. You are educating the buyer on the
new working with buyers paradigm.

Chantal continued her buyer listing presentation:

**Ms. Buyer, it is my company policy to work for you
exclusively in your upcoming real estate purchase. That
way, I can find you the perfect property for the price you
want to pay and with the terms that you can best afford.
How does that sound to you?**

Wait for the buyer to respond. The buyer will typically
say that it sounds good to them.

**Ms. Buyer, I want to give you some information
about real estate brokerage services. This will take just a
few minutes. After you see this information, I think you
will agree that what will be in your best interest is for me
to represent you exclusively in the purchase of your next
home. Would you like to see this information?**

Wait for the buyer to respond. If the buyer answers yes,
then continue with your presentation. If the buyer answers no
or maybe, then stop the presentation. Find out what is going
on with the buyer. It may be that the buyer lost focus or she
did not understand the question. If so, repeat what you said
and ask the question again.

The buyer may answer no because the buyer is aware of the
agency information involved in brokerage services. The buyer
may want to skip that step and want you to move on. That is
perfectly acceptable. Move on. So let's say Ms. Buyer says yes to
the would you like to see more information question.

**Ms. Buyer, in a real estate transaction, the seller can
be represented, the buyer can be represented, or the seller
and buyer can be represented. While there are several
different combinations of representation that may occur,
I prefer to keep it simple. I will exclusively represent you
as the buyer in the purchase of your next home. Would
that be all right with you?**

Wait for the buyer to respond. If the buyer answers yes,
then continue with your presentation. If the buyer answers no
or maybe, then stop the presentation. Again, find out what is
going on with the buyer. It may be that the buyer lost focus
or she did not understand the question. If so, repeat what you
said and ask the question again.

We have never had a buyer say no once the buyer understood the question. Real estate buyers want you to exclusively represent them. Real estate buyers want to receive value for the money they are spending for their real estate purchase.

Where Are We?

Let's see where we are before we move on to the next chapter. You have set a buyer listing appointment. You have prepared for the appointment. At the appointment, you have handled the logistics. So far, you are saying all the right things at the appointment.

In the next chapter, we will continue our buyer's listing presentation. We will show you how to you ask for a commitment from the buyer. We will talk further about what buyer listing agreement you are going to use. And we will discuss the length of the listing period you are going to ask for.

CHAPTER 7

How to Be Paid Every Time You Work with Buyers

In this chapter, we will continue our buyer listing presentation. We will show you how to ask for a commitment from the buyer. We will talk further about what buyer listing agreement you are going to use. And we will discuss the length of the listing period you are going to ask for.

We will also show you how to be paid every time you work with buyers. We think that as a real estate professional you should make at least $100 per hour working with buyers. But first things first.

To guarantee payment for services rendered, you must complete your successful buyer listing presentation. Once you have a signed buyer listing agreement, you can start the clock.

Where We Are

Let's see where we are in making the listing presentation to our buyer. We have set a buyer listing appointment. We have prepared for the appointment. At the appointment, we have handled the logistics. So far, we are saying all the right things at the appointment.

Let's rejoin Chantal and Ms. Buyer. Chantal is giving agency disclosure and planting the seeds for the buyer to have

Chantal exclusively represent her in the buyer's next real estate purchase. Chantal has just said the following in her buyer listing presentation to Ms. Buyer:

Ms. Buyer, in a real estate transaction the seller can be represented, the buyer can be represented, or the seller and buyer can be represented. While there are several different combinations of representation that may occur, I prefer to keep it simple. I will exclusively represent you as the buyer in the purchase of your next home. Would that be all right with you?

Let's assume that Ms. Buyer says yes, it would be all right with her.

Asking the Buyer for a Commitment

So far, every step in the buyer's listing presentation has been designed to elicit a commitment from the buyer. You are actually asking the buyer to make two commitments. The first commitment you are asking the buyer to make is a commitment to themselves. The second commitment you are asking the buyer to make is a commitment to you as their exclusive buyer's real estate agent.

The Buyer's First Commitment

Remember our trial closes from the last chapter? This is the time in the presentation to bring out your calendar and use a trial close.

Trial Closes
Mr. Buyer, if we decide to do business, do you have your calendar handy? I would like to find out your availability to look at property this week.

Ms. Buyer, do you have your calendar handy? I would like to find a convenient time for you to speak to a loan representative. That way, we can get you prequalified for the best home you can afford.

Mr. and Mrs. Buyer, I will have time on Tuesday to find the perfect property for you. Would you be available to see it on Wednesday afternoon or Thursday afternoon?

The idea is to use one of the trial closes. Each trial close is designed to have the buyer make a commitment to themselves. This is the commitment to themselves to buy real estate. If the buyer is not committed to themselves to buy real estate, this is the time for you to find this out.

Your Job

Your job will be to have the buyer make the commitment to themselves to buy real estate. Then if you can not get them to make this commitment, you need to end the buyer listing presentation. Otherwise, you will be wasting your time. If the buyer has no commitment to themselves to buy real estate, the buyer will have no commitment to you.

Chantal used the second trial close.

Ms. Buyer, do you have your calendar handy? I would like to find a convenient time for you to speak to a loan representative. That way, we can get you prequalified for the best home you can afford.

If Ms. Buyer gets her calendar, this gives you an indication that she is committed to herself to buy her next home. She has thought about the financial commitment involved in making a real estate purchase. By talking to a loan representative, the buyer will be putting that commitment into action. She and Chantal will know what is realistic as far as the price range of properties to look at.

If the buyer does not get her calendar, you need to find out what is going on. It may be as simple as the buyer did not understand you were asking her to get her calendar. Repeat the trial close.

Ms. Buyer, do you have your calendar handy? I would like to find a convenient time for you to speak to a loan representative. That way, we can get you prequalified for the best home you can afford.

If the buyer declines to get her calendar at this point, then your job will be to get the buyer to make the commitment to herself to buy real estate. Chantal would ask the following question:

Ms. Buyer, are you committed to buying your next home?

If Ms. Buyer says yes, then Chantal would say the following:

Ms. Buyer, I know the commitment it takes on your part to make this decision to buy your next home. I can appreciate that making this kind of commitment is not easy. Do you have your calendar handy?

If Ms. Buyer says no, then Chantal would say the following:

Ms. Buyer, I have successfully worked with literally hundreds of buyers. What I have learned is that unless you are committed to making a real estate purchase, nothing I can say or do will change your mind.

I suggest we get back together when you are sure that buying your next home is what you want to do. I appreciate you taking the time to invite me into your home. When would you like me to return so we can continue the process of finding your next home?

Chantal is doing a takeaway from Ms. Buyer. Unless you can get Ms. Buyer to make a commitment to herself to buy her next home, you really have to be prepared to walk out the door at this point of the buyer listing presentation. Otherwise, you are doing yourself and the buyer a disservice.

If Ms. Buyer asks you to stay and continue the presentation, do so only after you have received a positive response to these two questions.

Ms. Buyer, do you have your calendar handy?
Yes.

Ms. Buyer, would it be more convenient for you to speak with a loan representative on Wednesday morning or Thursday afternoon?
Thursday afternoon.

Pause: What Some of You May Be Thinking

Some of you may be thinking at this point that you can not follow our script. You may think it will not work for you or your buyers. That is fine with us. If you have a script that works for you and your buyers, that is great. Use your script.

We are sharing with you what we know works in a buyer's listing presentation.

We reiterate again. Just be clear that you can not wing your buyer's listing presentation. We are not interested in hearing you complain that after winging it you can not get buyers to sign buyer listing agreements with you. What we are sharing with you here works. We invite you to do what works.

The Buyer's Second Commitment

The second commitment you are asking the buyer to make is a commitment to you as their exclusive buyer's real estate agent. At this point, you have confirmed that the buyer is committed to themselves to buy real estate.

After Chantal has Ms. Buyer get her calendar and schedule the prequalifying call with the loan representative, she will continue with the buyer listing presentation. Let's see what Chantal will say next to Ms. Buyer.

Ms. Buyer, as I have already said, in a real estate transaction the seller can be represented, the buyer can be represented, or the seller and buyer can be represented.

While there are several different combinations of representation that may occur, I prefer to keep it simple. I will exclusively represent you as the buyer in the purchase of your next home. Would that be all right with you?
Yes.

Agency Disclosure

You have already had the buyer say yes to this question earlier in your buyer listing presentation. This will elicit a second yes from the buyer. Now is the time to bring out the real estate agency disclosure form for your area. In California, this form is called Disclosure Regarding Real Estate Agency Relationships. In Texas, this form is called Information about Brokerage Services.

You are going to have the buyer sign this disclosure form acknowledging receipt of this form. This is preparing the buyer to sign the buyer listing agreement later in the buyer listing presentation.

Ms. Buyer, I am going to give you a copy of our state-mandated real estate agency disclosure. I will need you to acknowledge receiving a copy of this agency disclosure form. Please sign and date the agency disclosure form where indicated.

Chantal has Ms. Buyer sign and date the agency disclosure form. Make sure you give a copy of the signed agency disclosure form to Ms. Buyer. This is part of eliciting the second commitment from Ms. Buyer. This commitment is Ms. Buyer making a commitment to you as her exclusive buyer's real estate agent.

The Buyer Listing Agreement

Now is the time we are going to talk about which buyer listing agreement you are going to use. To make a smooth transition to the buyer listing agreement, we recommend talking to the buyer about what types of property you can find for them. This will help cement the buyer's commitment to using you as their exclusive buyer's agent.

Types of Property You Can Find the Buyer

Let's rejoin Chantal and Ms. Buyer.

Ms. Buyer, before I talk about the exact benefits and features you want in your next home, I would like to share with you the types of property that I can find for you. Would that be all right with you?

Yes.

Ms. Buyer, you are going to love this! Once we have determined the exact benefits and features you want in your new home, I can show you any property that is available for sale.

This includes the property that is seller-listed with my company and property seller-listed by other brokers.

It would also include for-sale-by-owner property and new housing developments!

Ms. Buyer, I can also find you the perfect property once I know in writing what kind of property you want, even if that property is not on the market! Are you ready to get started?

Yes.

Types of Buyer Listing Agreements

We have said that the California Association of Realtors produces at least five types of buyer listing agreements. These include a buyer broker agreement—exclusive, a buyer broker agreement—nonexclusive, a buyer broker agreement—nonexclusive/not for compensation, a buyer nonagency agreement, and a disclosure/consent for representing more than one buyer!

Find a Buyer Listing Agreement

The types of buyer listing agreements will vary by your area or state. Your job is to find the buyer listing agreement that works for you. First, check your company policy with regard to what buyer listing agreement your company wants you to use.

If you are the broker and want to find a buyer listing form, check first with your local association of realtors, then your state association or your state licensing department. Whatever form you decide to use, we recommend you use a buyer listing agreement that has you exclusively represent the buyer.

Back to Chantal and Ms. Buyer

Chantal will now place the buyer broker agreement on the kitchen table. Most of the buyer broker agreements we have seen have very little space on the form to detail the exact nature of the property that the buyer wants to acquire.

For example, the California Association of Realtors buyer broker agreements have two blank lines to describe the property to be acquired. Chantal will therefore also place a blank piece of paper on the kitchen table.

Ms. Buyer, we are now going to put in writing the exact property you want me to find for your next home. After we fill this blank piece of paper with all the benefits and features you want in your next home, we will attach it to our buyer broker agreement. Would that be all right with you?

Yes.

This is the fun and exciting part of the buyer listing presentation. After you have spent whatever amount of time is necessary to put down on paper the exact property Ms. Buyer wants, then it is time to complete the rest of the buyer broker agreement.

Ms. Buyer should be so engaged in the process of creating her next home with you that there is no question in her mind that you are the real estate agent she wants to work with to find that property. Now you move on to the buyer broker agreement. This is when to start filling in the blanks.

Length of the Buyer Listing Period

One of the first areas to complete on whatever buyer listing agreement you are using is the length of the buyer listing period. The truth of the matter is that the buyer listing period could be for an afternoon. It could be for one year. Or it could be for any period of time in between!

Usually with seller listings, you want to get the longest listing period possible. Typically, six months to one year is ideal. That way, you have the seller and the property under exclusive contract for a long enough period of time. You may need that time for the property to be successfully marketed, shown, offers negotiated, and escrow closed.

With buyers, you can skip the marketing phase. You just have to show property, negotiate offers, and close escrow. This should take no more than three to six months. However, we do not recommend you take six-month buyer listings.

90 Days

We recommend you take 90-day buyer listings. We have found that we can find the exact property, negotiate an accepted offer, and close escrow within 90 days. This process can happen very quickly once you have a committed buyer.

You do not serve the buyer or yourself if you drag the process out for six months or longer. Buyers want to buy now. After all, they are going to have to move. You will be surprised how quickly things proceed in the new working with buyers paradigm once you have a signed buyer listing agreement.

Ms. Buyer, now that we have put down on paper the exact property you want me to find for you, we can complete the buyer broker agreement. I recommend we get started tonight and have you living in your next home within 90 days. Would that be all right with you?

Yes.

Compensation to Broker

Now comes our favorite part of the buyer listing agreement. We said at the beginning of this chapter that we would show you how to be paid every time you work with buyers. This is the part of the buyer listing agreement in which you are guaranteed payment for services rendered.

Every state will have some statutory writing about the amount of real estate commissions. California requires the following verbiage under the compensation to broker portion of the California Association of Realtors buyer broker agreement.

NOTICE: The amount or rate of real estate commissions is not fixed by law.

What this means is that you can negotiate any compensation package you want with the buyer. It can be a percentage of the purchase price. It can be a percentage of the purchase price and a dollar amount. It can be just a dollar amount. It can be an hourly fee.

Make at Least $100 per Hour

We think that as a real estate professional you should make at least $100 per hour working with buyers. The median price for a home in California is more than $500,000. A seller listing at 6 percent would generate a $30,000 commission.

Seller Paid Commission

Purchase Price	$500,000
Commission Percentage	× 6%
Commission Amount	$30,000

If you sold that property for $500,000 as a cooperating broker in the old working with buyers paradigm, you would typically make 3 percent, or $15,000.

Cooperating Broker Commission

Purchase Price	$500,000
Commission Percentage	× 3%
Commission Amount	$15,000

In the new working with buyers paradigm, if you negotiated with the buyer a fee of $100 per hour, you would have to work 150 hours to make $15,000.

Number of Hours to Make $15,000

Commission Amount	$15,000
Hourly Compensation	$100
$15,000 / $100 per Hour = 150 Hours	

You would have to work almost four 40-hour weeks (160 hours). Our point is that in the old working with buyers paradigm, you do not feel one pang of guilt making a $15,000 commission selling a buyer a $500,000 property. Why should you feel guilty in the new working with buyers paradigm making $100 per hour? You are going to work hard for your money.

Let's see how Chantal is doing.

Ms. Buyer, the next part of the agreement is the compensation to broker section. I as your broker will work for you exclusively. My fee is 3 percent of the purchase price. If I can negotiate the seller paying my fee, I will do so. Any fees that the seller pays will be credited against the 3 percent fee you are agreeing to pay. Would that be all right with you?

Yes.

The buyer says no.

What if the buyer says no, it would not be all right with them to pay you a 3 percent fee in the event you can not negotiate the seller paying your fee? What do you say? Remember, you are still in the education business.

You have to educate the buyer that the buyer is always the party in a real estate transaction that pays the real estate commission. We said in Chapter 2 that the combination of the buyer's down payment and their ability to obtain new financing was the source of the funds for completing the real estate transaction, including paying the real estate commission.

We invite you to use the illustration on the next page to help you educate the buyer on how real estate commissions work. We call this the Circle Talk. Use the following script as you present the Circle Talk to the buyer.

Circle Illustration Demonstrating the Buyer Paying Real Estate Commissions

Circle Talk Script

Ms. Buyer, let me show you how real estate fees and commissions are paid in a real estate transaction. Were you are aware that the buyer pays all of the real estate commissions?

No

Ms. Buyer, let me show you something.

Take out the Circle Talk illustration.

The combination of the buyer's down payment and the buyer's ability to obtain new financing is the source of the funds for completing every real estate transaction, including paying the real estate commissions.

Write *down payment* and *new financing* in the space above Buyer. This would be the top left quadrant of the circle between the Buyer and Seller (see Figure 7.1a).

Ms. Buyer, have you heard the expression *follow the money?*

Yes.

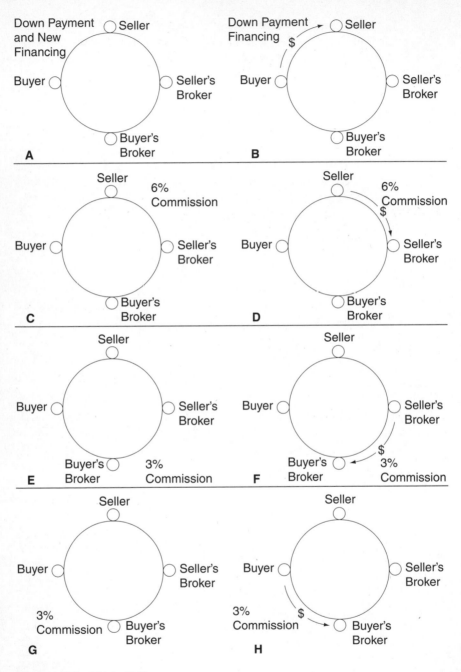

Figure 7.1 Circle Talk.

Ms. Buyer, let's follow the money.

Draw a curved line above the arc of the circle from the Buyer's circle to the Seller's circle. Write a dollar sign on the curved line halfway in between. Then add arrows at the Seller circle to indicate that the money is going from the Buyer to the Seller (see Figure 7.1b).

Ms. Buyer, all the money from your down payment and the proceeds from your new loan go to the Seller's side of the escrow. Out of this money, the Seller has to pay off any existing Seller loans and all the Seller expenses associated with the closing. This includes real estate commissions the Seller has agreed to pay.

Write 6 percent in the space above Seller's Broker. This would be the top right quadrant of the circle between the Seller and Seller's Broker (see Figure 7.1c).

Ms. Buyer, typically the real estate commission the Seller agrees to pay the Seller's Broker is 6 percent.

Draw a curved line above the arc of the circle from the Seller's circle to the Seller's Broker circle. Write a dollar sign on the curved line halfway in between. Then add arrows at the Seller's Broker circle to indicate that the 6 percent real estate commission is going from the Seller to the Seller's Broker (see Figure 7.1d).

Ms. Buyer, again typically the Seller's Broker will split that 6 percent real estate commission 50/50 with the Buyer's Broker.

Write 3 percent in the space below Seller's Broker. This would be the bottom right quadrant of the circle between the Seller's Broker and Buyer's Broker (see Figure 7.1e).

Ms. Buyer, the Seller's Broker would keep 3 percent of the real estate commission. The Buyer's Broker will receive the other 3 percent of the real estate commission.

Draw a curved line, in this case below or outside the arc of the circle from the Seller's Broker circle to the Buyer's Broker circle. Write a dollar sign on the curved line halfway in between. Then add arrows at the Buyer's Broker circle to indicate that the 3 percent real estate commission is going from the Seller's Broker to the Buyer's Broker (see Figure 7.1f).

Ms. Buyer, can you see when we follow the money that you as the buyer in the transaction are actually the source of the money that is paying the real estate commissions to the Seller's Broker and to the Buyer's Broker?

Yes.

Write 3 percent in the space below Buyer. This would be the bottom left quadrant of the circle between the Buyer and Buyer's Broker (see Figure 7.1g).

Ms. Buyer, what I am proposing is that you pay my fee directly to me rather than you paying my fee in the circuitous manner I have just described.

Draw a curved line, in this case below or outside the arc of the circle from the Buyer circle to the Buyer's Broker circle. Write a dollar sign on the curved line halfway in between. Then add arrows at the Buyer's Broker circle to indicate that the 3 percent real estate commission is going from the Buyer to the Buyer's Broker (see Figure 7.1h).

Ms. Buyer, would that be all right with you?

We think that after you educate the buyer with the Circle Talk, the buyer will understand that the buyer is paying your real estate commission. Then it is a relatively simple matter to complete the buyer listing agreement.

Ms. Buyer, now that you understand that you are paying my 3 percent fee, we are just about finished. I would like you to please acknowledge that you have read, received a copy of, and agree to the terms of this agreement. Would that be all right with you?

Yes.

Congratulations. You have just completed a successful buyer listing presentation. You now know the secret to being paid every time you work with buyers. The secret is to represent buyers exclusively and have them agree to pay you for services rendered.

In the next chapter, we will show you how to ask for and receive retainers from buyers. This will complete the design of the new working with buyers paradigm. We will tell you how much of a retainer to ask for. We will also tell you how to get a nonrefundable retainer. This is starting to sound very professional. Would that be all right with you?

CHAPTER 8

How to Ask for and Receive Retainers from Buyers

I n this chapter, we show you how to ask for and receive retainers from buyers. We will recommend how much of a retainer to request. We will also tell you how to get a nonrefundable retainer. Once we have finished this chapter, we will have completed the design of the new working with buyers paradigm.

How to Ask for a Retainer

You have to make a business decision when it comes to asking buyers for a retainer. Some of you may decide that in the new working with buyers paradigm, your comfort zone is having the buyer sign any type of buyer listing agreement. Just the fact that a buyer has agreed to work with you exclusively may be enough to have you on the road to doubling your commissions working with buyers.

For those of you who may be a bit bolder, you may decide that in the new working with buyers paradigm, having buyers sign an exclusive buyer listing agreement wherein the buyer agrees to pay you a real estate commission will have you doubling your commissions working with buyers.

For those of you who want to embrace the new working with buyers paradigm completely, asking buyers for a retainer will come as a natural part of the package. You will ask for a retainer as part of the buyer listing presentation.

Ask for a Retainer during the Buyer Listing Presentation

Let's go back into the buyer listing presentation. We are going to show you at what point in the presentation to ask for a retainer. We will start with the section on the compensation to broker. Let's rejoin Chantal and Ms. Buyer.

Ms. Buyer, the next part of the agreement is the compensation to broker section. I as your broker will work for you exclusively. My fee is 3 percent of the purchase price. If I can negotiate the seller paying my fee, I will do so. Any fees that the seller pays will be credited against the 3 percent fee you are agreeing to pay. Would that be all right with you?

Yes.

Ms. Buyer, in order for me to get started, I request a nonrefundable retainer fee of one-half of 1 percent (0.5%). This would be $1,500 based on the price range you are looking in. This fee is compensation for our initial professional consultations, for my researching potential properties, and for my putting together the plan and the resources to have you living in your next home within 90 days from today. Would that be all right with you?

Yes.

Nonrefundable Retainer

Price Range	$300,000
Percentage of Retainer	$\times$ 0.5%
Retainer Amount	$1,500

The Buyer Says No

What if the buyer says no, it would not be all right with them to pay you a nonrefundable retainer fee of one-half of

1 percent (0.5%)? What do you say? You are still in the education business. Again, you have to educate the buyer that it is in the buyer's best interest to have you represent them in the purchase of their next home. Let's replay the scenario.

Ms. Buyer, in order for me to get started I request a nonrefundable retainer fee of one-half of 1 percent (0.5%). This would be $1,500 based on the price range you are looking in. This fee is compensation for our initial professional consultations, for my researching potential properties, and for my putting together the plan and the resources to have you living in your next home within 90 days from today. Would that be all right with you?

No.

Then Chantal would say.

Ms. Buyer, the retainer is credited against the 3 percent fee you are already agreeing to pay. Would that be all right with you?

Yes.

What if the buyer says no? Let's replay that last part.

Ms. Buyer, the retainer is credited against the 3 percent fee you are already agreeing to pay. Would that be all right with you?

No.

Ms. Buyer, the retainer will be deposited into my broker trust account. I will be giving you a weekly accounting of my activities on your behalf. Would that be all right with you?

Yes.

What if the buyer still says no? Let's replay again.

Ms. Buyer, the retainer fee will be deposited into my broker trust account. I will be giving you a weekly accounting of my activities on your behalf. Would that be all right with you?

No.

Chantal will now ask this question.

Ms. Buyer, what is it about the retainer that is not all right with you?

I am not comfortable writing you a check for the retainer tonight.

This Means One of Three Things

This answer means one of three things. The first thing it may mean is that the buyer does not have the money to write you a check for the full $1,500 retainer. Once you determine this is the case, then this can be easily handled on your part. Ask the buyer when they would be able to write you a check for the retainer?

Ms. Buyer, I understand that you do not have the money to write me a check for the retainer tonight. When would it be all right for you to write me a check for the retainer?

As in any sales situation when you have asked the client a question, keep your mouth shut. Let the client answer the question. The client will tell you what she is prepared to do. Let's look at some of the client's possible answers.

Possible Client Answers

I can write you a check next week.

We have found that if the buyer makes a commitment to write a check for the retainer to you within seven days of the buyer listing appointment, the buyer will usually do so.

I can write you a check in two weeks.

If the buyer says she can not write a check for the retainer until more than seven days from the listing appointment, the buyer will most likely never write you a check.

I can write you two checks tonight. You can cash one of the checks for $750 tomorrow. Please hold onto the second check of $750 till next week.

The buyer may feel comfortable writing you a check for $750 that is good immediately. And the buyer may feel comfortable writing you a check for the other $750 that she asks you to hold for a week. This has worked for us.

Let's go back to Chantal's question.

Ms. Buyer, what is it about the retainer that is not all right with you?

I am not comfortable writing you a check for the retainer tonight.

The Buyer Is Not Serious about Buying

The second thing that it may mean is that if the buyer will not pay you a nonrefundable retainer, the buyer is not serious about buying. We say how can the buyer be serious about buying if the buyer will not come up with 0.5 percent of the purchase price to give you a retainer?

Using the numbers we have talked about so far, you are asking the buyer to come up with $1,500 for the retainer. What makes you think the buyer is going to come up with $300,000 at the closing if the buyer does not come up with $1,500 to get the transaction started?

Asking for a retainer gives you another opportunity to close the buyer on the buyer's commitment to herself to buy her next home. Once you determine that the reason the buyer is not comfortable writing you a check for the retainer tonight is because the buyer's commitment to herself to buy her next home is wavering, again ask the following question:

Ms. Buyer, are you committed today to buying your next home?

Yes.

Ms. Buyer, I know the commitment it takes on your part to make this decision to buy your next home. You can make your commitment real by giving me a retainer. I can appreciate that making this kind of commitment is not easy. Do you have your checkbook handy?

Yes.

We have found that 9 times out of 10 we have been able to have the buyer recommit to buying their next home. Then they write the retainer check. Do not let the buyer off the hook if the buyer says no. You will be doing the buyer and yourself a disservice if Ms. Buyer really wants to buy her next home.

If Ms. Buyer says no, then Chantal would again do a takeaway.

Ms. Buyer, as I have said, I have successfully worked with literally hundreds of buyers. What I have learned is that unless you are committed to making a real estate purchase, nothing I can say or do will change your mind.

I suggest we get back together when you are sure that buying your next home is what you want to do. I appreciate

you taking the time to invite me into your home. When would you like me to return so we can continue the process of finding your next home?

Next week.

Ms. Buyer, I would be happy to return next week. However, I think you have already made up your mind. Right now, are you really sure that buying your next home is what you want to do or is it really not what you want to do. Which is it?

If Ms. Buyer tells you she now is really sure that buying her next home is what she wants to do, go right back to the question at hand.

Ms. Buyer, I am happy to hear that you are really sure buying your next home is what you want to do now. Do you have your checkbook handy?

Yes.

If Ms. Buyer tells you she is now really sure that buying her next home is what she does not want to do, pull the plug on your buyer listing presentation while leaving the door open to do business in the future.

Ms. Buyer, I am glad that as a result of my presentation, you have been able to determine that buying your next home now is something you do not want to do. I am sure that very soon you will determine that buying your next home is what you want to do.

I will gladly be willing to be of assistance to you at that time. Thank you for the opportunity to come into your home. Are there any friends or family members that you know that are thinking about buying or selling real estate?

Always ask for referrals. You have been completely professional with Ms. Buyer. She may be completely sold on you as a real estate professional. She just has not sold herself on buying her next home.

The Buyer Is Not Committed to You

The third thing it may mean is that if the buyer will not pay you a nonrefundable retainer, then the buyer is not committed to you as her exclusive buyer's agent. Asking for a retainer gives you another opportunity to close the buyer on the buyer's commitment to you as her exclusive buyer's agent.

Once you determine that the reason the buyer is not comfortable writing you a check for the retainer is because the buyer's commitment to you as her exclusive buyer's agent is wavering, you need go back to that part of the listing presentation.

Ms. Buyer, as I have already said, in a real estate transaction the seller can be represented, the buyer can be represented, or the seller and buyer can be represented.

While there are several different combinations of representation that may occur, I prefer to keep it simple. I will exclusively represent you as the buyer in the purchase of your next home.

Ms. Buyer, I have given you a copy of our state-mandated real estate agency disclosure form. You have acknowledged receiving a copy of this agency disclosure form. You said it would be all right with you for me to represent you exclusively in the purchase of your next home.

Now you want to ask the following question:

Ms. Buyer, do you still want me to represent you exclusively in the purchase of your next home?

Yes.

Ms. Buyer, do you have your checkbook handy?

Yes.

It may be just as simple as that. By going back into the listing presentation and giving people the same information for a second or third time, we have found it makes it easier for people to digest that information.

What if Ms. Buyer says no?

Ms. Buyer, do you still want me to represent you exclusively in the purchase of your next home?

No.

Ms. Buyer, would you please share with me why not?

This is where the cat comes out of the bag.

I am uncomfortable having you represent me exclusively because _____.

Top Four Objections

1. *What if I am not happy with you and want to find another agent? I will not be able to do that if I sign an exclusive buyer listing agreement with you.*
2. *My father/mother/sister/brother is a real estate agent. After you find a property that I like, I am going to have my family member licensee write the offer.*
3. *I think it would be better to have many real estate agents looking for property for me rather than just you looking for property for me.*
4. *What if I change my mind and decide not to buy another home? After all, my financial circumstances could change for the worse.*

Handling Objections

Now you have objections that have been voiced by Ms. Buyer. Once you have heard these objections, then you have the opportunity to deal with them. It is much better to handle these objections now rather than later in the transaction.

If you can not handle the objections now, it will be better for you and Ms. Buyer not to do business. So let's handle the objections one at a time. Remember, we are again closing the buyer on being committed to you as her exclusive buyer's agent.

Objection 1

1. *What if I am not happy with you and want to find another agent? I will not be able to do that if I sign an exclusive buyer listing agreement with you.*

Ms. Buyer, it is true that once you sign an exclusive buyer listing agreement with me you will not be able to work with another agent until our listing agreement expires. Are you happy with me so far?
Yes.

Ms. Buyer, do you remember all the letters of recommendation from some of my very happy clients that I
showed you?

Yes.

Ms. Buyer, I promise you that I will make you
another one of my very happy clients. Would that be all
right with you?

Yes.

Ms. Buyer, after we close escrow on your next home
and you are one of my very happy clients, will you write a
letter of recommendation for me?

Yes.

Ms. Buyer, do you have your checkbook handy?

Yes.

Again, it may be just as simple as that. By going back
into the listing presentation and giving people the same information for a second or third time, we have found it makes it
easier for people to digest that information.

What if Ms. Buyer says no?

Ms. Buyer, do you have your checkbook handy?

No.

This may be the point where you have to end the buyer
listing presentation. Ms. Buyer may not be willing to sign
an exclusive buyer listing agreement that includes writing a
check for a nonrefundable retainer. Again, you want to do a
takeaway while leaving the door open to do business in the
future.

Ms. Buyer, I am glad that as a result of my presentation, you have been able to determine that buying your
next home now is something you want to do. I know that
from successfully working with hundreds of buyers that
exclusively representing you in the real estate transaction
will make you happy.

When you decide that you would like me to exclusively represent you in your next home purchase, I
will gladly be willing to be of assistance to you at that
time. Thank you for the opportunity to come into your
home. Are there any friends or family members who
you know who are thinking about buying or selling real
estate?

Objection 2

2. My father/mother/sister/brother is a real estate agent. After you find a property that I like, I am going to have my family member licensee write the offer.

Ms. Buyer, I appreciate you being honest with me. I assume that because you are talking to me that your father/mother/sister/brother works part-time in the real estate industry. Is my assumption correct?
Yes.

Ms. Buyer, I can appreciate you wanting to work with a family member. However, buying real estate in today's market is a very complicated business. One mistake could cost you your financial future. Do you really want to trust a part-timer, albeit a family member, with the biggest financial commitment of your life?
No.

Ms. Buyer, do you have your checkbook handy?
Yes.

What if Ms. Buyer says no?

Ms. Buyer, do you have your checkbook handy?
No.

This may be another point at which you have to end the buyer listing presentation. Ms. Buyer may not be willing to sign an exclusive buyer listing agreement that includes writing a check for a nonrefundable retainer because of the family licensee connection. Again, you want to do a takeaway while leaving the door open to do business in the future.

Ms. Buyer, I am a full-time real estate professional. I have successfully worked with hundreds of buyers exclusively representing them in their real estate transactions. Your family member licensee may have the best of intentions regarding your next home purchase.

Ms. Buyer, let's say you needed a major medical operation. Let me ask you a question. Would you have it done by a part-time surgeon even if the surgeon was a family member or would you have it done by a full-time surgeon?
I would have it done by a full-time surgeon.

Ms. Buyer, when you decide that you would like a full-time real estate professional to exclusively represent you in your next home purchase, I will gladly be willing to be of assistance to you at that time. Thank you for the opportunity to come into your home.

Just so you know, we have both had buyers who had family members that were part-time real estate licensees. Both of us have had buyers who were in that situation sign exclusive buyer listing agreements and give us nonrefundable retainers after we asked the part-time versus full-time surgeon question.

Objection 3

3. *I think it would be better to have many real estate agents looking for property for me rather than just you looking for property for me.*

Ms. Buyer, do you remember that I shared with you the types of property that I could find for you?
Yes.

Ms. Buyer, do you remember that this included the property that is seller-listed with my company and property seller-listed by other brokers?
Yes.

Ms. Buyer, do you remember that it also included for-sale-by-owner property and new housing developments?
Yes.

Ms. Buyer, do you remember that I also said that once we have determined the exact benefits and features you want in your new home, I can show you any property that is available for sale?
Yes.

Ms. Buyer, do you remember that I also said that I can find you the perfect property once I know in writing what kind of property you want, even if that property is not on the market?
Yes.

Ms. Buyer, are you ready to get started?
Yes.
Ms. Buyer, do you have your checkbook handy?
Yes.
Although this might seem like overkill, we think you get our point. We have demonstrated to the buyer that we can find the perfect property for them. We have become Ms. Buyer's one-stop real estate buyer's shop.

Objection 4

4. *What if I change my mind and decide not to buy another home. After all, my financial circumstances could change for the worse.*

Ms. Buyer, I understand that your financial circumstances could change for the worse. Are you planning for that to happen in the next 90 days?
No.
Ms. Buyer, do you have your checkbook handy?
Yes.
What if Ms. Buyer says no, but what if they did?
Ms. Buyer, I understand that your financial circumstances could change for the worse. Are you planning for that to happen in the next 90 days?
No, but what if they did?
Let's reply.
Ms. Buyer, I am going to be your fiduciary as well as your real estate agent. That means I have to do everything for you that is in your best interest financially.

If that means that it is in your best interest not to go through with your next home purchase because your financial circumstances change for the worse, then I will help you do just that. Would that be all right with you?
Yes.
Ms. Buyer, do you have your checkbook handy?
Yes.

Ms. Buyer Loses Her Job

Let's say Ms. Buyer loses her job after signing a buyer listing agreement and giving you a nonrefundable retainer of $1,500. You have been working with Ms. Buyer for three weeks. In that period of time you have spent an average of five hours per week specifically working for Ms. Buyer. You have 15 hours into this transaction.

You have been diligently researching potential properties. You have made contact with your former buyers who may want to sell their homes to Ms. Buyer. You have checked for-sale-by-owner web sites and classified ads. You have let your builder contacts know about Ms. Buyer's home requirements.

You have personally previewed 11 homes. You have shown Ms. Buyer 5 of those homes. You have had 12 to 15 e-mails and/or phone calls with Ms. Buyer. You have sent an additional 19 e-mails and made an additional 17 phone calls on Ms. Buyer's behalf. This is not to mention the two-hour professional counseling and real estate education you provided Ms. Buyer at the buyer listing appointment.

Then you receive the frantic phone call from Ms. Buyer informing you that she has lost her job and no longer has an interest in buying her next home. You commiserate with Ms. Buyer and let her know that you will put finding her next home on hold.

Ms. Buyer Wants Her Retainer Back

Ms. Buyer than asks you if you will refund her $1,500 non-refundable retainer. You tell Ms. Buyer no. Then you review with Ms. Buyer all the work you have done on her behalf. We recommend you put this in writing and send a copy to Ms. Buyer.

You suggest that you keep the buyer listing agreement going just in case Ms. Buyer finds another job in the immediate future. You let Ms. Buyer know that you will transfer credit for the retainer to a buyer listing agreement you put together in the future if she winds up not buying her next home during the current buyer listing agreement period.

In this chapter, we showed you how to ask for and receive retainers from buyers. Now that we have finished this chapter, we have completed the design of the new working with buyers paradigm. You will never work with buyers for free again.

In the next chapter, we will show you how to represent buyers. We have touched on a key point at the end of this chapter about how to represent buyers. You become a fiduciary of the buyer once the buyer listing agreement is signed. Operating out of the new working with buyers paradigm makes you a real estate professional with buyers. Now it is time to act like one.

CHAPTER 9

Representing Buyers

In this chapter, we will show you how to represent buyers. Representing buyers will double the amount of the real estate commissions you made in the old working with buyers paradigm. Operating out of the new buyers paradigm makes you a real estate professional with buyers. Now is the time to start acting like one.

We touched on a key point at the end of the last chapter about how to represent buyers. We said you become a fiduciary of the buyer once the buyer listing agreement is signed.

Fiduciary means of, pertaining to, or acting as a trustee. One who holds something in trust. As a fiduciary of the buyer, you put the buyer's best interest first. You act as a trustee protecting the buyer's best interest.

You Are a Fiduciary of the Buyer

Our caveat, as we look at representing buyers, is there is not enough room in this book to cover the specific information available in every state. We think that you can find out your state specifics by accessing your state's agency disclosure forms.

Once we finished our research, we realized that there are consistencies in the intent, whereas the wording used may vary slightly from state to state. We have used examples from places that most closely represent all the states. Having said that, let's take a look at how Texas and California regard you if you are the broker who represents the buyer.

Texas

According to the Information about Brokerage Services that is Approved by the Texas Real Estate Commission for Voluntary Use:

If the Broker Represents the Buyer

The broker becomes the buyer's agent by entering into an agreement to represent the buyer, usually through a written buyer representation agreement. A buyer's agent can assist the owner but does not represent the owner and must place the interests of the buyer first. The owner should not tell a buyer's agent anything the owner would not want the buyer to know because the buyer's agent must disclose to the buyer any material information known to the agent.

What is interesting to us about this form is directly under the line at the top that says "Approved by the Texas Real Estate Commission for Voluntary Use" are the following lines in teeny-tiny type:

Texas law requires of real estate licensees to give the following information about brokerage services to perspective buyers, tenants, sellers, and landlords.

So is the information voluntary to be given by real estate licensees or required to be given by real estate licensees to prospective clients? This form is obviously influenced by the old working with buyers paradigm.

Also, did you notice the paragraph talks about owners not disclosing information to the buyer's agent. The law requires the disclosure be given to prospective sellers and not prospective owners.

Finally, even though everything is couched in the old working with buyers paradigm, two things stand out.

1. A buyer's agent . . . must place the interests of the buyer first.
2. The buyer's agent must disclose to the buyer any material information known to the agent.

You Are a Fiduciary of the Buyer

In Texas, once you have a signed buyer listing agreement, you are a fiduciary of the buyer. You must place the interests of your buyer first. Notice the use of the word *must*. When you see the word *must*, it means there are no exceptions. This means you must place the interests of your buyer above your interests.

As the buyer's agent, you must disclose to the buyer any material information you know. Again notice the use of the word *must*. Any material information you know could and should include canceling the transaction if it is not in the buyer's highest and best interest to go through with the purchase.

Real Estate Agents Exploit Their Informational Advantage

The track record of the real estate industry carrying out its fiduciary duties to sellers, let alone buyers, is not good, however. The National Bureau of Economic Research, which is a Cambridge, Massachusetts, think tank, issued working paper number 11053 in January 2005.

The paper was entitled "Market Distortions When Agents Are Better Informed: The Value of Information in Real Estate Transactions" by Steven Levitt and Chad Syverson. This paper was reviewed by Linda Gorman.

Evidence Is Damning

The evidence against the real estate industry is damning. The authors examined data on 98,000 suburban Chicago home sales from the Multiple Listing Service of Northern Illinois. As many of you know, the National Association of Realtors is headquartered in Chicago.

Thirty-three hundred of the 98,000 homes were owned by real estate agents. The authors found that the real estate agents selling their own homes behaved differently than when they were representing sellers as fiduciaries.

After controlling for property location, property charac-
teristics, and property conditions, the real estate agent–owned
homes stayed on the market almost ten days longer and sold
for 3.7 percent more than comparable homes owned by sellers
who hired real estate agents to represent them!

Additional Profit

A 3.7 percent higher sales price on a $300,000 home means
an additional $11,100 in gross profit.

Additional Profit

Home Selling For	$300,000
Higher Sales Percentage	× 3.7%
Additional Profit	$11,100

By waiting 10 days, the seller would net an additional
$10,434 after subtracting the additional 6 percent commis-
sion on the additional profit of $11,100.

Additional Commission

Additional Gross Profit	$11,100
Additional Commission Percentage	× 6%
Additional Commission	$666

Seller's Net

Additional Gross Profit	$11,100
Additional Commission	− $666
Seller's Net	$10,434

Agent Incentive

The authors further point out that real estate agents receive
only a small share of the additional profit when a seller's
home sells for a higher price. The real estate agent representing the seller, typically a salesperson getting half of the

3 percent commission coming to the seller's listing broker, would net another $167.

"Unless the costs for an additional week of listing the home are less than $167, the agent has an incentive to urge the homeowner to forgo waiting for what could be a substantially higher offer." In other words, the agent has an incentive to convince their sellers to sell their homes too cheaply and too quickly.

Real estate agents selling their own homes received both their commission and the homeowner's share. "Given the commission structure, the finding that agent-owned homes are on the market longer and sell for more suggests that agents do deploy their specialized knowledge to maximize their profits rather than those of the homeowners they represent."

Real Estate Industry Paradigm

Yikes! It appears that this study indicates that real estate agents exploit their informational advantage at the expense of their clients. This does not sound like these real estate agents are meeting their fiduciary duties to their clients.

Our position is that it is the real estate industry paradigm that is at the root of the problem and not bad or unscrupulous real estate agents. We say the real estate industry paradigm skews the fiduciary relationship between sellers and their real estate agents. How skewed, then, is the fiduciary relationship between buyers and their real estate agents?

California

According to the Disclosure Regarding Real Estate Agency Relationships as required by the California Civil Code, a buyer's agent in California is defined as:

Buyer's Agent

A selling agent can, with the Buyer's consent, agree to be the agent for the Buyer only. In these situations, the agent is not the Seller's agent, even if by agreement the agent may receive compensation for services rendered, either in full or in part from the seller. An agent acting only for the Buyer has the following affirmative obligations:

To the Buyer:

A fiduciary duty of utmost care, integrity, honesty and loyalty in dealings with the Buyer.

To the Buyer and the Seller:

(a) Diligent exercise of reasonable skill and care in performance of the agent's duties.
(b) A duty of honest and fair dealing and good faith.
(c) A duty to disclose all facts known to the agent materially affecting the value or desirability of the property that are not known to, or within the diligent attention and observation of the parties.

An agent is not obligated to reveal to either party any confidential information obtained from the other party, that does not involve the affirmative duties as set forth above.

Like with the Texas agency disclosure, two things stand out for us with the California disclosure.

1. To the Buyer:

A fiduciary duty of utmost care, integrity, honesty and loyalty in dealings with the Buyer.

2. To the Buyer and the Seller:

An agent is not obligated to reveal to either party any confidential information obtained from the other party, that does not involve the affirmative duties as set forth above.

You Are a Fiduciary of the Buyer

We certainly started off well in number 1. Once you have a signed buyer listing agreement, you are a fiduciary of the buyer in California. You must place the interests of your buyer first. However, we seem to lose part of the mantle of being a fiduciary of the buyer in number 2.

Unlike in Texas, the California law does not hold you as the buyer's agent to the "must disclose to the buyer all material information you acquire" standard. For example, as a buyer's agent in California, you are not obligated to tell the buyer the seller told you in confidence that the seller would take a lower price for their property.

In Texas, because of your fiduciary relationship, you must disclose this information to your buyer. Too bad the seller told you in confidence that he would take a lower price. You are a 100 percent fiduciary of the buyer. You are a 0 percent fiduciary of the seller.

Skewed Again

From where we sit, it looks like California has put you as a real estate agent in less than a 100 percent fiduciary relationship with your buyer. That is the case even if you and the buyer have signed an exclusive buyer listing agreement.

Again, you are stuck in the crosshairs of the real estate industry paradigm that skews the relationship between buyers and their real estate agents. Agency disclosure was supposed to clear up the question "Whose agent are you?" Unfortunately, agency disclosure typically creates more problems than it solves.

It may look like the Texas real estate industry is ahead of the California real estate industry as far as clarifying that a buyer's agent owes a 100 percent fiduciary relationship to the buyer. However, the real estate industry in Texas has its own problems.

Federal Trade Commission

As we were writing this book, the Federal Trade Commission charged the Austin Board of Realtors with illegally restraining competition. According to a Federal Trade Commission release dated July 13, 2006, the Austin Board of Realtors (ABOR) was required to eliminate its 2005 rule blocking Internet searches for nontraditional low-cost brokerage properties.

> "ABOR's Web site rules create significant roadblocks for real estate brokers to offer consumers alternatives to full service brokerage agreements," said Jeffrey Schmidt, Director of the FTC's Bureau of Competition. "By its law enforcement action today, the commission is not saying that one form of brokerage agreement is better than another. We are saying that the consumer should be able to decide."

Now for those of you who think this has nothing to do with buyer representation, please reconsider. The Federal Trade Commission is telling the Texas Legislature (Austin is the state capital) and the Texas real estate industry to take care of the real estate consumer, The real estate consumer is a real estate seller or a real estate buyer.

An Agency Relationship Is in the Consumer's Best Interest

An agency relationship is in the consumer's best interest. When you are in a true agency relationship with the consumer, you become a 100 percent fiduciary of the consumer. Only when you are a 100 percent fiduciary of the consumer can you truly represent the consumer.

The Federal Trade Commission was telling the Austin Board of Realtors and by extension the state of Texas that if you are in an agency relationship, you are in a fiduciary relationship. The Austin Board of Realtors was negating its professed fiduciary relationship with the real estate consumer by putting the interests of full-service real estate brokers ahead of the real estate clients they were supposed to be representing.

Representing Real Estate Buyers

We have said that buyers are the true real estate consumer. The buyers are the ones with the money. It makes sense to us that you would want to take very good care of the people who have the money. They are paying your commission.

It also makes sense to the people who have the money that they should be taken care of by their real estate agents. Buyers want you to take care of them. The basis of taking care of real estate buyers is to have a fiduciary relationship with them.

By having a 100 percent fiduciary relationship with buyers, you have a professional relationship with buyers. We recommend you start acting like a real estate professional with buyers starting now.

Overrepresent Buyers

We think that you want to overrepresent buyers rather than underrepresent buyers. What we mean when we say we want you to overrepresent buyers rather than underrepresent buyers is to go beyond the minimum acceptable standard of compliance with your state's real estate laws.

We have mentioned already in this chapter that the Federal Trade Commission has become very active enforcing antitrust laws against the real estate industry. This is a trend that is going to continue.

The enforcement effort so far has been against the real estate industry and its anticonsumer paradigm. Soon it will be against individual companies. Then it will be against individual real estate agents. We recommend you get ahead of this curve. After all, do you want to spend time in the gray bar motel?

Ahead of the Curve

How do you get ahead of the curve? Let's look at some examples of how to represent buyers in the new working with buyers paradigm.

Example 1

You are working with a buyer under the terms of a buyer listing agreement.

The buyer has agreed to pay you a 3 percent commission based on the purchase price the buyer pays for the property.

The property the buyer is interested in making an offer on is on the market for $550,000. You discover in talking with the seller during a preview of the property that the seller will sell the property for $500,000.

You show the property to your buyer. Your buyer wants to make an offer on the property. The buyer wants you to write an offer for $525,000. As a fiduciary of the buyer, what should you do?

Dilemma

You know that if you write the offer for $525,000, the seller will accept that offer in a heartbeat. You will make a 3 percent commission on $525,000, or $15,750.

Your Commission

Buyer Pays	$525,000
Commission Percentage	× 3%
Your Commission	$15,750

However, if you share with your buyer the information that the seller will take $500,000 for the property, you will lose $750 in commission. Instead of making a $15,750 commission you will only make a $15,000 commission.

Your Commission

Buyer Pays	$500,000
Commission Percentage	× 3%
Your Commission	$15,000

Pop quiz: What do you do? You would be respecting the wishes of your buyer if you wrote the offer for $525,000. The buyer might even be quite happy with the deal when the seller accepted the $525,000 offer.

If you wrote the offer for $525,000, would you be representing the buyer as a fiduciary? The answer is clearly no. You would be putting your interests of getting a higher commission above the buyer's interests of getting a better deal.

As a fiduciary representing the buyer, your job is to inform the buyer about the information you gleaned from the seller that the seller would sell the property for $500,000. You write the offer for $500,000.

Transaction in California

If this transaction were taking place in California, it could be argued that you did not have to tell your buyer what the seller said regarding what the seller would accept as a purchase price. This would be an argument for underrepresenting the buyer as far as we were concerned.

We would recommend you overrepresent your buyer as in the action you took of informing your buyer what the seller told you. If push came to shove and you wound up in court being sued by your buyer for whatever reason, your best defense is you were a fiduciary of the buyer in every act of commission and every act of omission you made.

Example 2

Let's take up where we left off in example 1. You write the offer for $500,000. You are feeling good about yourself. You have been a 100 percent fiduciary for your buyer. You present the offer to the sellers. Mrs. Seller says she will not take one penny less than $525,000! You look over at Mr. Seller. He grins sheepishly at you from across the table and shrugs his shoulders.

You take the counteroffer for $525,000 back to your buyer. The buyer asks you what happened. You tell the buyer that Mrs. Seller said she would not sell for one penny less than $525,000. Mr. Seller, who was the one who told you he would take $500,000 for the property, was clearly not in charge of the negotiations.

Your buyer says that they will accept the $525,000 counteroffer. After all, that was what they were planning on paying for the property to begin with. You just made another $750 commission. You made that extra commission the right way. You were a true fiduciary for your buyer.

Example 3

The principal is responsible for the acts of their agent. This is a two-way street conversation that is very poorly understood by the real estate industry. Once an agency relationship has been created, the principal and the agent are held to that agency relationship.

This agency relationship can be an expressed-in-writing relationship through a buyer listing agreement, which is what we are recommending. This agency relationship can be implied by the actions of the principal and their agent with no written agreement in place.

The implied agency relationship is the old working with buyers paradigm at its worst. We are strongly recommending you do not operate out of this old working with buyers paradigm ever again. Here is why.

Let's say you are working with a buyer and you have no signed buyer listing agreement in place. You give the buyer your state-mandated agency disclosure. You and the buyer agree that you will exclusively represent the buyer in any real estate transaction. So far, so good.

In-House Listing

You show the buyer a property that is listed by another agent in your office. Your buyer is interested in the property. You write an offer and present the offer to the seller at the seller's kitchen table. You are there. The seller is there. The other agent in your office who has the property listed is there. The buyer is not there.

Conspiracy Table

You present the offer. The seller and listing agent ask you to step outside so they can talk privately. When they invite you back inside, they have prepared a counteroffer for you. Again, so far, so good.

You take the counteroffer back to your buyer. Your buyer is not happy with the counteroffer. Your buyer is not happy with you. Your buyer accuses you of working for the seller's best interest and not the buyer's best interest.

Lawsuit

The buyer sues you in court, claiming you violated your fiduciary duty to the buyer. The buyer claims you conspired with the seller and the seller's listing agent to have the buyer pay a higher price for the property. The buyer claims this occurred at the seller's kitchen table when the offer was presented.

The buyer's attorney argues the seller was present, the seller's agent was present, and you were present. The only one not present was the buyer. The three of you conspired at the seller's kitchen table to have the buyer pay a higher price for the property. You did not carry out your fiduciary duty.

Does this sound far-fetched? These kinds of lawsuits are already happening. Maybe you have been sued since you have been in the real estate business. Maybe you know someone in the real estate business who has been sued. Although you are being sued personally, the attack is on the real estate industry paradigm.

Protect Yourself

The best way to protect yourself is to have written buyer listing agreements. Then you must take on being a representative of your buyer in a 100 percent fiduciary capacity. This is the best way to refute the real estate industry paradigm that is anticonsumer. It is also the best way to double your commissions working with buyers.

In the next chapter, we will talk about dual agency. Dual agency is the ultimate bastion of the real estate industry's anticonsumer paradigm. If you sell one of your seller listings to one of your buyers, you make twice the commission. But you take on twice the risk trying to serve two masters.

We believe that dual agency will become unlawful to practice as a real estate agent in the next ten years. We think that entities like the Federal Trade Commission, state attorneys general, state real estate licensing boards, and the courts will mount a concerted attack on the practice of dual agency in real estate transactions.

That is why we think it is imperative for the real estate industry to get out in front of this issue. Dual agency can still be practiced as a transition office policy. By creating a new working with buyers paradigm, we as an industry can eliminate dual agency.

The real estate industry will be able to take the lead in being proconsumer. We will make more money. We will avoid being sued. We will be regarded as professionals. Representing buyers as fiduciaries is the crucial first step.

CHAPTER 10

Dual Agency

I n this chapter, we will talk about dual agency. Dual agency is the ultimate bastion of the real estate industry's anti-consumer paradigm. If you sell one of your seller listings to one of your buyers, you make twice the commission. But you take on twice the risk trying to serve two masters.

Obviously, there is not room in this book to cover the specific information available in every state on dual agency. We think that you can find out your state specifics by accessing your state's agency disclosure forms.

Once we finished our research, we realized that there are consistencies in the intent, whereas the wording used may vary slightly from state to state. We have used examples from places that most closely represent all the states.

We believe that dual agency will become unlawful to practice as a real estate agent in the next ten years. That is why we think it is imperative for the real estate industry to get out in front of this issue. By creating a new buyers paradigm, we as an industry can eliminate dual agency.

What Is Dual Agency?

Dual agency is being the agent of more than one principal at the same time. The biggest proponent of dual agency is the real estate industry. It is part and parcel of the real estate industry paradigm of having a professional relationship with sellers and having an unprofessional relationship with buyers.

We have said the real estate industry has a professional relationship with sellers because the use of seller listing agreements is standard throughout the real estate industry. We have said the real estate industry has an unprofessional relationship with buyers because the use of buyer listing agreements is sporadic throughout the real estate industry.

Fraught with Peril

The concept of dual agency is fraught with peril. Let's say you went to see an attorney to have the attorney sue someone for you. As you are sitting in the attorney's waiting room, you see the person you want to sue walk out of the attorney's office.

You enter the attorney's office and remark that the person who just walked out is the person you want the attorney to sue. The attorney looks up from her desk and says, "No problem." The person you want to sue wants the attorney to help them sue you!

The attorney has agreed to be the attorney for the person you want to sue to sue you! Then the attorney says she would be glad to be the attorney to help you sue that same person.

Besides making your head hurt, isn't this the most ridiculous thing you have ever heard? Your attorney is going to represent you and the person you are suing at the same time in the same lawsuit. This will never happen.

Twice the Reward, Twice the Risk

What we have just described happens every day in every part of the real estate world in real estate transactions. Real estate agents represent both the buyer and the seller in the same real estate transaction. This has twice the reward for the agent. It also has twice the risk.

How is it possible for the real estate agent representing both the seller and the buyer to get the highest price and best terms for the seller in the transaction and the lowest price and best terms for the buyer in that same transaction? The answer is it is not possible for that to happen. The best you can hope for is a compromise.

The Buyer Loses

The real estate agent who is the dual agent makes twice the commission. The dual agent receives the seller listing agent commission and the buyer selling agent commission. Even these terms are confusing.

The principal who consistently loses financially in these transactions is the buyer. The buyer is the principal in the transaction with the money. The seller is the principal in the transaction with the equity. As we have said, without the buyer there is no real estate market.

We know that in today's normal real estate market, many of you have lots of seller listings that are costing you money to market. We also know that it is taking two to three times as long for you to find a buyer to buy your listings as it did two years ago.

Dual Agency in California

Dual agency is alive and well in California. Historically, California has always been the trendsetter when it comes to the real estate industry. Unfortunately, this is not the case with dual agency. Dual agency is firmly entrenched in the California real estate industry paradigm.

Let's look at what the California Association of Realtors Disclosure Regarding Real Estate Agency Relationships form says about dual agency.

Agent Representing Both Seller and Buyer

A real estate agent, either acting directly, or through an associate licensee can legally be the agent of both the Seller and the Buyer in a transaction, but only with the knowledge and consent of both the Seller and the

Buyer. In a dual agency situation, the agent has the following affirmative obligations to both the Seller and the Buyer:

(a) A fiduciary duty of utmost care, integrity, honesty, and loyalty in the dealings with either the Seller or the Buyer.

Our Comments

Let's stop here to comment. How can, in a dual agency situation, the real estate agent have an affirmative obligation to a fiduciary duty of utmost care, integrity, honesty, and loyalty in the dealings with either the seller or the buyer?

In the section on being a Seller's Agent, the California Disclosure Regarding Real Estate Agency Relationships states the agent has:

A fiduciary duty of utmost care, integrity, honesty and loyalty in dealings with the Seller.

In the section on being a Buyer's Agent, the California Disclosure Regarding Real Estate Agency Relationships states the agent has:

A fiduciary duty of utmost care, integrity, honesty and loyalty in dealings with the Buyer.

We understand and agree with the wording that you have a fiduciary obligation to the seller when you are a seller's agent. We understand and agree with the wording that you have a fiduciary obligation to the buyer when you are a buyer's agent.

What makes no sense to us is how you can have the exact same fiduciary obligation with either the seller or the buyer at the same time? Even the wording describing the fiduciary obligation you have is exactly the same for seller's agent, buyer's agent, and agent representing both seller and buyer.

A fiduciary duty of utmost care, integrity, honesty, and loyalty in the dealings with either the Seller or the Buyer.

Definition of Fiduciary

We have said a dictionary definition of *fiduciary* means of, pertaining to, or acting as a trustee. One who holds something in trust. As a fiduciary of the seller, you put the seller's best interest first. You act as a trustee protecting the seller's best interest. As a fiduciary of the buyer, you put the buyer's best interest first. You act as a trustee protecting the buyer's best interest.

California Definition of Fiduciary

So let's say the California definition of fiduciary is different from what the dictionary says is the definition of fiduciary. And let's say you can have a California fiduciary duty of "utmost care, integrity, [and] honesty . . . in the dealings with either the Seller or the Buyer" in a dual agency relationship.

Major Problem
We have a major problem with the California definition of fiduciary, which is used in all three agency disclosures for the seller, the buyer, and both the seller and the buyer. Our major problem is with the use of the word *loyalty*.

A fiduciary duty of utmost . . . loyalty in the dealings with either the Seller or the Buyer.

A fiduciary duty of utmost loyalty should certainly be the case when you are the seller's agent under any definition of fiduciary. A fiduciary duty of utmost loyalty should certainly be the case when you are the buyer's agent under any definition of fiduciary.

How is it possible to have a fiduciary duty of utmost loyalty with either the seller or the buyer at the same time in the same transaction? You know, like in writing the offer with your buyer. You are being loyal to the buyer when you write the offer the way the buyer wants you to write it.

Offer for Less Than the Seller's Asking Price

But how are you being loyal to the seller if you write the offer for less than the seller's asking price for the property? What about when the seller wants you to write a counteroffer? You are being loyal to the seller when you write the counteroffer the way the seller wants you to write it. But how are you being loyal to the buyer if you write the counteroffer for more than the buyer's original offer for the property?

Loyalty = Trust

In Chapter 14, "Buyer Loyalty," we will devote that chapter to showing that buyer loyalty is a two-way street. You are loyal to your buyers and your buyers are loyal to you because you trust them and they trust you.

There is no loyalty or trust possible in a California dual agency real estate transaction between the buyer's agent and the buyer. For that matter, there is no loyalty or trust possible in a California dual agency real estate transaction between the seller's agent and the seller. So what do you do?

Dual Agency Can Still Be Practiced as a Transition Office Policy

Dual agency in California can still be practiced as a transition office policy. To protect yourself under current California Disclosure Regarding Real Estate Agency Relationships, you must comply with the following:

> You can start off exclusively representing the seller and can bring on board the buyer and be a dual agent.
> You can start off exclusively representing the buyer and can bring on board the seller and be a dual agent.
> As the seller listing agent, you give agency disclosure to the seller.

As the buyer listing agent, you give agency disclosure to the buyer.

As the buyer listing agent, you give agency disclosure to the seller when you present the buyer's offer.

Dual Agency in Texas

Dual agency in Texas is on its way out. This is a step in the right direction. In fact, Texas no longer uses the term *dual agency*. Texas uses the term *intermediary*. In the Texas Real Estate Commission Information about Brokerage Services form, dual agency is not even mentioned.

If the Broker Acts as an Intermediary

A broker may act as an intermediary between the parties if the broker complies with the Texas Real Estate Licensee Act. [This means the broker is duly licensed by the state of Texas to be a real estate broker.] The broker must obtain the written consent of each party to the transaction to act as an intermediary. The written consent must state who will pay the broker, and . . . set forth the broker's obligations as an intermediary. The broker is required to treat each party honestly and fairly.

Intermediary

An intermediary acts as a mediator or go-between for the parties. In the Texas Real Estate Commission world, the real estate broker acting as an intermediary is an agent of neither the seller nor the buyer.

A broker who acts as an intermediary in a transaction:

(1) shall treat all parties honestly;
(2) may not disclose that the owner will accept a price less than the asking price unless authorized in writing to do so by the owner;

(3) may not disclose that the buyer will pay a price greater than the price submitted in a written offer unless authorized in writing to do so by the buyer; and

(4) may not disclose any confidential information or any information that a party specifically instructs the broker in writing not to disclose unless authorized in writing to disclose the information or required to do so by the Texas Real Estate License Act or a court order or if the information materially relates to the condition of the property.

The Texas category of the broker acting as an intermediary when the broker brings both parties to the real estate transaction seems to avoid the inherent problems of dual agency. However, it still does not address how to take care of the seller or the buyer in a fiduciary manner when only one broker is involved in the transaction.

We will revisit dual agency and the broker as intermediary in Chapter 17, "The Future of the Real Estate Industry." For now, let's get back to our discussion of dual agency. We are going to look at California and the dual agency dilemma one more time.

Dual Agency in California Revisited

To be fair with California and the California real estate industry, we must revisit dual agency in California. California has been grappling with agency disclosure and dual agency for fifteen years. What has California come up with?

Rather than coming up with a new working with buyers paradigm, the California Association of Realtors has spent much time and money figuring out how to keep the old working with buyers paradigm in place. So far, it has been time and money well spent as far as the advocates of the old paradigm are concerned.

The key element has been protecting seller-listing brokers and their ability to sell their own listings. As in every state, brokers in California prefer that sellers sign written exclusive seller listing agreements. This automatically creates an agency relationship between the listing agent and the seller.

Looks Like Consumer Choice

What looks like consumer choice for the buyer in California becomes an overwhelming information overload. The overload starts with the two-page Disclosure Regarding Real Estate Agency Relationships. Page 1 delineates the seller's agent, the buyer's agent, and the agent representing both the seller and the buyer agency relationships.

Page 2 for the first half of the page is written in little tiny legalese boilerplate that gives you a headache just looking at it. Then, in the middle of the page, there are two blank lines that are to be filled with the names of the real estate brokers involved in the transaction at this point.

The first blank line has "Name of Listing Agent" written underneath it. That seems neutral enough. It could mean the name of the seller's listing agent. It could mean the name of the buyer's listing agent. No such luck. It is strictly for the seller's listing agent.

The second blank line has "Name of Selling Agent (if not the same as the Listing Agent)." Oh, this must mean the name of the buyer's listing agent. Unless of course the buyer is not being represented.

Then when you look more closely, you realize that whatever "name of listing agent" is written onto line 1 "is the agent of (check one)"

The seller exclusively; or both the buyer and seller.

Let's see. The listing broker preference is to have the seller sign an exclusive authorization and right-to-sell listing agreement. We said this automatically creates an agency relationship between the listing agent and the seller. But the seller's listing agent can dump representing the seller exclusively and also agree to be the agent of the buyer through a dual agency relationship.

No Consumer Choice

The seller listing agent just has to inform the seller that the seller listing agent is also going to represent the buyer in the real estate transaction. The seller listing agent does this by giving the seller another Disclosure Regarding Real Estate Agency Relationships checking the box *both the buyer and seller.*

The seller has no choice if that is what the seller agent wants to do. This is starting to sound like Texas and the Austin Board of Realtors under the gun of the Federal Trade Commission's antitrust division for their anticonsumer stance toward sellers. Of course, it does not get any better when you look at what follows line 2.

Whatever "name of selling agent if not the same as the listing agent" is written onto line 2 "is the agent of (check one)"

The buyer exclusively; or the seller exclusively; or both the buyer and seller.

More Buyer Choices?

Wow, it looks like the buyer has even more choices, three, than the seller's two. The selling agent, who we would say in the new paradigm is the buyer's agent, can represent the buyer exclusively, the seller exclusively, and can be a dual agent of both the buyer and the seller.

Does anyone else think something strange is going on here? The selling agent representing the buyer exclusively can dump representing the buyer exclusively and also agree to be the agent of the seller through a dual agency relationship.

Although that is strange enough, it is parallel to what the listing agent can do. What is completely strange is that the selling agent can exclusively represent the seller! What is going on here? What looks like more consumer choice for the buyer turns out to be no choice.

The California Association of Realtors solution is to not represent the buyer at all! The selling agent, who is different from the listing agent, can check the box that the selling agent is going to represent the seller exclusively in the transaction. This surely handles the dual agency problem.

This is the old working with buyers paradigm at its nastiest. It says we will show you buyer liars, buyer flakes, and buyer lookie-loos. You are not even worth being represented by us in a real estate transaction. The seller is king and queen for us in the current real estate industry paradigm.

Federal Trade Commission Problem

Again we say, the real estate industry has a professional relationship with sellers because the use of seller listing agreements is standard throughout the real estate industry. Again we say, the real estate industry has an unprofessional relationship with buyers because the use of buyer listing agreements is sporadic throughout the real estate industry.

This will be the basis of the Federal Trade Commission moving forward against the real estate industry for being anti-consumer. The fact that it is possible for a buyer not to be represented in California and elsewhere throughout the country is the Achilles' heel of our industry.

Buyer Listing Agreements Become Standard

Our solution is to make buyer listing agreements standard across the real estate industry. This would immediately handle the anticonsumer bias the real estate industry has against buyers. It would certainly handle the problem we have been looking at in California.

Handle the California Problem
The California Association of Realtors Disclosure Regarding Real Estate Agency Relationships form has only two possible boxes to check for listing agent. That is because once you have a signed seller listing agreement, you can never abandon

an agency relationship with the seller completely. At worst, the listing agent becomes a dual agent representing both the seller and the buyer.

There are three possible boxes to check, however, if you are the selling agent. The box saying the selling agent is representing the seller exclusively is not possible if the selling agent has a signed buyer listing agreement. We call on the California Association of Realtors to take the lead in eliminating the selling agent being able to represent the seller exclusively.

Never Abandon the Buyer Completely

Once you have a signed buyer listing agreement, as with the signed seller listing agreement, you can then never abandon an agency relationship with the buyer completely. At worst, the selling agent becomes a dual agent representing both the seller and the buyer.

In the next chapter, we will talk about divided agency. We have said that dual agency is fraught with peril. We say this because dual agency can easily be regarded as divided agency.

If one of the parties to a real estate transaction brings an action claiming that the real estate agents involved in the transaction practiced divided agency, the agents could be in big trouble. Once divided agency is proved, the remedy for divided agency is splitting the deal apart after it has closed escrow.

The real estate agents will be forced to disgorge their commission. *Disgorge* is a technical term meaning "give back." The real estate agents can be disciplined by their state real estate licensing authority. They can be sued for damages in civil court.

The real estate agents can be prosecuted in criminal court for deceptive trade practices and fraud. We say it this way: The difference between dual agency and divided agency is five years in the gray bar motel!

This chapter and the next chapter are our "we are trying to frighten you" chapters. We want to convey to you the dangers of continuing to operate in the old real estate industry paradigms of working with sellers and working with buyers. Consider these two chapters as a wake-up call.

CHAPTER 11

Divided Agency

Again, remember there is no room in this book to cover specifics from each state, so we used examples from places that most closely represent all the other states. In this chapter, we will talk about divided agency. Divided agency is pure peril. Both for the real estate client(s) and for the real estate agent(s) involved in a divided agency transaction.

Once divided agency is proved, one of the possible court-imposed remedies for divided agency is splitting the deal apart. This could happen after an offer has been accepted and before the deal goes into escrow. This could happen during the escrow period. The deal could even be split apart after escrow has closed!

The most perilous outcome for real estate clients involved in a divided agency transaction is the deal being split apart after escrow has closed. The seller probably has moved out of the property. The buyer has probably moved into the property.

The negative outcome for the real estate agent(s) involved in a divided agency transaction is being forced to disgorge their commission, being disciplined by their state real estate licensing authority up to and including losing their real estate license(s), and being sued for damages in civil court. The real estate agent(s) can even be prosecuted in criminal court for deceptive trade practices and fraud. If the real estate agent(s) is found guilty, the punishment could include being fined and/or going to prison.

Divided Agency

What is divided agency? Divided agency is being an agent of more than one principal in a real estate transaction without the knowledge and consent of all the principals involved in that real estate transaction.

Example 1

Let's say you are an associate licensee in your company. You meet with a buyer. You do not do a buyer listing presentation. You do not put together a written buyer listing agreement with this buyer.

You give the buyer your state's required agency disclosure. You tell the buyer you are exclusively working for them. You have the buyer sign your state's required agency disclosure and give them a copy.

Company Policy

Your company policy is to exclusively represent the buyer when the buyer is buying another broker's seller listing. Your company policy is to exclusively represent the seller when anyone in your company brings the buyer that buys one of your broker's seller listings.

You find several properties to show your buyer. Some are seller-listed with different real estate companies. Some are seller-listed with your company. The buyer likes a property that is seller-listed with a different real estate company.

You write an offer and present it to the seller and the associate licensee of the other real estate company who took the seller listing. The seller accepts your buyer's offer. Congratulations, you have put a deal together. Or have you put a deal together?

Unilateral Offer of Subagency

Every real estate broker that is a member of their board's or association's Multiple Listing Service accepts a seller-listing broker's offer of subagency. This is by default if you are a member of a Multiple Listing Service. You are automatically working for the seller as a subagent of the seller's listing broker.

You must refute the seller's listing broker's unilateral offer of subagency at the offer presentation if you are exclusively representing the buyer in the transaction. If you do not refute the unilateral offer of subagency at the offer presentation, you are in a divided agency situation.

Dual Agency Not Automatic

In our scenario, you are not automatically in a dual agency situation. You started off giving your buyer your state's required agency disclosure. You then told the buyer that you were exclusively working for the buyer. You have even checked that you were exclusively representing the buyer on the offer-to-purchase paperwork.

We said in the last chapter on dual agency that you must take proactive measures to make sure you are in a dual agency position.

> You can start off exclusively representing the seller and you can bring on board the buyer and be a dual agent.
> You can start off exclusively representing the buyer and you can bring on board the seller and be a dual agent.
> As the seller listing agent, you give agency disclosure to the seller.
> As the buyer listing agent, you give agency disclosure to the buyer.
> As the buyer listing agent, you give agency disclosure to the seller when you present the buyer's offer.

So you have started off exclusively representing the buyer and you can bring on board the seller and be a dual agent. Then you would avoid being in a divided agency situation.

In order to do this, you must take two proactive measures. As the buyer listing agent, you give agency disclosure to the buyer *and* as the buyer listing agent you give agency disclosure to the seller when you present the buyer's offer.

Complied with the First Proactive Measure

You have complied with the first proactive measure when you gave agency disclosure to the buyer. This is the case even though you do not have a written buyer's listing agreement in place. The requirement is only to give agency disclosure to the buyer.

You present the offer to the seller and fail to give the seller agency disclosure. You have not complied with the second proactive measure necessary to establish dual agency. So what is the problem? There is now a divided agency situation. How, you ask?

Act of Omission

Your act of omission has created the divided agency. You have not refuted the unilateral offer of subagency. You are an agent of the seller and an agent of the buyer without the knowledge and consent of both parties. This is the definition of divided agency.

You refute the unilateral offer of subagency by complying with the second proactive measure. By giving the seller agency disclosure at the offer presentation, you establish that you are exclusively representing the buyer. This also establishes that the seller's listing agent is exclusively representing the seller. Now there is no dual agency, let alone divided agency.

What about the Offer?

What about the fact that you checked that you were exclusively representing the buyer on the offer to purchase? That protects you against divided agency, right? Actually, that is what has you in a divided agency situation!

By not refuting the unilateral offer of subagency when you are presenting the offer to the seller, you are automatically a subagent of the seller through the seller's listing broker by virtue of the Multiple Listing Service. You now have a divided agency situation with the buyer.

Because you are representing the buyer and you are representing the seller as a subagent without the knowledge and consent of the buyer, you are representing the seller by default through the unilateral offer of subagency.

What Is the Big Deal?

The big deal happens when the buyer decides for whatever reason that they are unhappy with their purchase. You know, when the buyer comes down with a case of buyer's remorse. And as we have said, some of these cases of buyer's remorse are terminal.

Buyer's Remorse

We are saying the buyer has a case of buyer's remorse because after they have closed escrow and moved in, the buyer decides they want their money back. The buyer contacts an attorney to explore ways to split the deal apart.

The attorney reviews the transaction with the buyer. The attorney looks at all the paperwork. The attorney tells the buyer the only way to split the deal apart is if the buyer's agent engaged in a divided agency practice.

The attorney tells the buyer that that may be likely if the buyer's agent did not refute the unilateral offer of subagency from the seller's broker. The buyer has no idea what the attorney is talking about. But the attorney has built his practice on demonstrating that real estate agents have engaged in divided agency.

Outcome 1

The buyer's attorney takes the case. The buyer's attorney files a lawsuit against the seller, the seller's listing broker, and the buyer's broker. Why is the attorney going after the seller and the seller's broker? Didn't we say that it was the buyer's broker who had practiced divided agency?

Major Forthcoming Area of Litigation

Divided agency is a major forthcoming area of litigation. Attorneys know that the practice of dual agency is on thin legal ice. When that ice cracks, everyone involved is in the frigid waters of divided agency.

The problem is that full disclosure is not being given by the real estate industry to their clients. Although we are focusing on developing a new working with buyers paradigm, the real estate industry's old working with sellers paradigm is also in need of a major paradigm shift.

Sellers Are Responsible

Sellers are not being told by the real estate industry that sellers as principals are responsible for the acts of their real estate agents. Real estate agents include the seller's listing agent as well as subagents. That means seller listing agents at the seller listing presentation are not giving full disclosure to the seller.

Full disclosure is beyond giving agency disclosure. Real estate agents are not disclosing the liability to the seller when they list the seller's property on the Multiple Listing Service. The liability arises for the seller because most Multiple Listing Services are unilateral offers of subagency.

Sellers are also not being told that they are responsible for the acts of their agents and subagents. Sellers can be sued as principals responsible for the acts of their agents and subagents. In our example, the buyer's agent is the subagent of the seller.

The seller is being sued by the buyer's attorney for the buyer's agent's act of omission in not refuting the unilateral offer of subagency. This is what created the divided agency. The seller is responsible for the buyer's agent's act of omission.

Seller's Listing Agent Sued

The buyer's attorney is suing the seller's listing agent for offering the buyer's agent a unilateral offer of subagency wherein the buyer's agent is automatically working as an agent of the seller. A smart attorney is also going to sue the local Multiple Listing Service that created the unilateral offer of subagency.

Are you starting to get a sense of why the buyer's attorney is suing the seller and the seller's listing broker along with the buyer's broker? All three are at fault along with the Multiple Listing Service for creating a divided agency.

Full Disclosure?

Let's look again at the California Association of Realtors Disclosure Regarding Real Estate Agency Relationships form.

Seller's Agent

A Seller's agent under a listing agreement with the Seller acts as the agent for the seller only. A seller's agent or a subagent of that agent has the following affirmative obligations . . .

This is the only mention of subagent on page 1 of the agency disclosure form. At the bottom of page 1 it says:

This disclosure form includes the provisions of Sections 2079.13 to 2079.24, inclusive of the Civil Code set forth on page 2. Read it carefully.

Written directly underneath the previous statement it says:

"I/WE ACKNOWLEDGE RECEIPT OF A COPY OF THIS DISCLOSURE AND THE PORTIONS OF THE CIVIL CODE PRINTED ON THE BACK (OR A SEPARATE PAGE).

Then the buyer and seller are supposed to sign with the date and time.

Page 2

We have already mentioned the problem with page 2. You know the boilerplate that is written in the itsy-bitsy type that gives you a headache. On page 2, the top third of the page quotes civil code section 2079.13 of the state of California.

This gives the definitions of the terms used on page 1, which is the so-called disclosure regarding real estate agency relationships. The last definition of the terms used on page 1 is definition (o) for subagent.

(o) Subagent means a person to whom an agent delegates agency powers. . . . However, subagent does not include an associate licensee who is acting under the supervision of an agent in a real property transaction.

Completely Clear

Probably 999 out of 1,000 real estate brokers (agents) are not clear about the definition of a subagent. Probably 9,999 out of 10,000 sales associates (associate licensees) are not clear about the definition of a subagent. And probably 99,999 out of 100,000 real estate sellers are totally unclear about subagents.

What is particularly distressing to us is that at the bottom of page 1 after the buyer and seller have signed that they have received a copy of the disclosure it says:

THIS FORM HAS BEEN APROVED BY THE CALIFORNIA ASSOCIATION OF REALTORS (C.A.R.). NO REPRESENTATION IS MADE AS TO THE LEGAL VALIDITY OR ADEQUACY OF ANY PROVISION IN ANY SPECIFIC TRANSACTION.

Totally Inadequate

By using the CAR form, you are using an agency disclosure form that is totally inadequate in terms of disclosure regarding subagency and the seller's liability as the principal for the actions of their agents and subagents. So what is the point of reading the disclosure form carefully?

And when you read the disclaimer, which appears as part of the boilerplate at the bottom of page 1 of the disclosure form, you realize that the CAR will not stand behind "the legal validity or adequacy of any provision in any specific transaction." Wow!

Texas Is No Better

The situation in Texas is really no better than the situation in California as far as the legal pitfalls surrounding divided agency for the real estate industry. Again, looking at the Texas

Information about Brokerage Services form, we find the following statement about subagents. (Please remember, you must check with the state you are operating in for the legalities regarding divided agencies. It is your job, and you will be held responsible.)

If the Broker Represents the Owner

The broker becomes the owner's agent by entering into an agreement with the owner, usually through a written listing agreement, or by agreeing to act as a subagent by accepting an offer of subagency from the listing broker. A subagent may work in a different real estate office. A listing broker or subagent can assist the buyer but does not represent the buyer and must place the interests of the owner first. The buyer should not tell the owner's agent [or subagent] anything the buyer would not want the owner to know because an owner's agent [or subagent] must disclose to the owner any material information known to the agent [or subagent].

We reiterate. Sellers are not being told that they are responsible for the acts of their subagents. Sellers can be sued as principals responsible for the acts of their subagents. In the old working with buyers paradigm, this would be the acts of the cooperating or selling broker.

Sellers are on the hook for the acts of their subagents whether these acts are acts of commission or acts of omission. Sellers are on the hook whether the seller has been given adequate and informed disclosure or not. And it is pretty clear that the sellers are not receiving adequate and informed disclosure.

The Difference between Dual Agency and Divided Agency

Using Texas as an example again, the last paragraph under IF THE BROKER ACTS AS AN INTERMEDIARY says:

With the parties' consent, a broker acting as an intermediary between the parties may appoint a person who is licensed under the Texas Real Estate License Act and associated with the broker to communicate with and carry out instructions of one party and another person who is licensed under that Act and associated with the broker to communicate and carry out instructions of the other party.

Broker = Agent

This makes it sound like when an associate licensee of the broker has the seller listing and another associate licensee of the broker has the buyer, we have handled the divided agency dilemma. But have we really? Actually, there is only one agent in this transaction.

Associate licensees are not agents for purposes of agency law or agency disclosure. Only the broker of record for a real estate company is an agent. So, although the Texas disclosure regarding *if the broker acts as an intermediary* tries to make it appear that there are two real estate "agents" involved in the transaction, there is really only one agent in an in-house real estate sale.

Example 2

Let's say you are an associate licensee in your company. You meet with a buyer. You do not do a buyer listing presentation. You do not put together a written buyer listing agreement with this buyer.

You give the buyer your state's required agency disclosure. You tell the buyer you are exclusively working for them. You have the buyer sign your state's required agency disclosure and give them a copy.

Company Policy

Your company policy is to exclusively represent the buyer when they are buying another broker's seller listing. Your company policy is to exclusively represent the seller when anyone in your office brings the buyer that buys one of your broker's seller listings.

You find several properties to show your buyer. Some are seller-listed with different real estate companies. Some are seller-listed with your company. The buyer likes a property that is seller-listed with your company.

You write an offer and present it to the seller and the associate licensee from your company who took the seller listing. The seller accepts your buyer's offer. Congratulations, you have put a deal together. Or have you put a deal together?

Problem

There is a seller agency relationship created when the associate licensee takes the listing between the seller and the broker of record. There is a buyer agency relationship when you as a different associate licensee have more than a casual relationship with the buyer. Writing an offer for the buyer qualifies as more than a casual relationship with the buyer.

Can of Worms

This real estate transaction has opened up a whole new can of worms. We are not talking about dual agency here. This is an in-house real estate sale. The company policy, we have said, is to exclusively represent the seller. There is only one agent in this transaction because both associate licensees work for the same broker.

You, as the associate licensee, write an offer on the property for the buyer. You inform the buyer that you are now exclusively representing the seller in the transaction. This appears odd to your buyer because there is another real estate licensee who is already representing the seller.

What happens if the buyer refuses to consent to giving up the buyer agency relationship with your broker to be exclusively represented in the real estate transaction? The answer is that it is not up to the buyer. It is only up to the broker. If the broker wants to exclusively represent the seller in the transaction, then the broker can exclusively represent the seller. In effect, the broker stops representing the buyer.

The buyer can still have the offer written and presented by you as the associate licensee. The buyer just will not be represented in the transaction.

If the buyer wants to be represented in the transaction, the buyer can go find another company to write the buyer's offer.

Outcome 2

Let's say the buyer goes through with the deal with you writing the offer as the associate licensee of the broker with the seller listing. The buyer even agrees that the broker is exclusively representing the seller and the buyer will be unrepresented by the broker in the transaction.

Another Pause

Can you imagine the broker in this transaction telling the seller the broker is going to dump the seller and exclusively represent the buyer? No, you cannot imagine this ever happening. The real estate industry paradigm will not allow it.

Buyer's Remorse

You know what happens next. The buyer decides for whatever reason that they are unhappy with their purchase. The buyer has buyer's remorse. After the buyer has closed escrow and moved in, the buyer decides they want their money back. The buyer contacts an attorney to explore ways to split the deal apart.

It's Attorney Time!
The attorney reviews the transaction with the buyer. The attorney looks at all the paperwork. The attorney tells the buyer that it looks like the deal can be split apart because the real estate company engaged in a divided agency practice.

The attorney tells the buyer that that may be likely because the buyer was told the buyer was being exclusively represented by you as the associate licensee. After you wrote an offer for one of your company's seller listings, you told the buyer that the buyer was no longer being represented by you in the transaction. In fact, the buyer was not being represented by anyone.

The attorney tells the buyer this was a classic case of bait and switch. The agent (the broker) was representing more than one party in the transaction without the knowledge and consent of all the parties. The buyer did not understand that the broker would be loyal to the seller and disloyal to the buyer. This is divided agency.

The buyer's attorney takes the case. The buyer's attorney files a lawsuit against the seller, the seller's listing broker, the associate licensee who took the seller listing, and you, the associate licensee who wrote the offer for the buyer.

North Carolina

In a final twist to wanting to keep dual agency alive and the old working with buyers paradigm in place, we give you one of the latest real estate industry variations. It is called designated agency. It is another case of divided agency waiting to happen.

Let's look at the North Carolina Association of Realtors, Inc., Working with Real Estate Agents disclosure form. Under the dual agency section of the seller's portion, the language is again completely incriminating:

> You may even permit the listing firm and its agents to represent you and a buyer at the same time. This "dual agency relationship" is most likely to happen if an agent with your listing firm is working as a *buyer's* agent with someone who wants to purchase your property. If this occurs and you have not already agreed to a dual agency relationship in your listing agreement, your listing agent will ask you to sign a separate agreement or document permitting the agent to act as agent for both you and the buyer.

And what is in this for the seller? If you say the listing firm is bringing a buyer, we say that was what the listing firm is supposed to do, according to the seller listing agreement. Why should the seller lose when the real estate company is supposedly doing its job? The next paragraph says:

It may be difficult for a *dual agent* to advance the interests of both the buyer and seller.

Really?

Nevertheless, a *dual agent* must treat buyers and sellers fairly and equally. Although the *dual agent* owes them the same duties, buyers and sellers can prohibit *dual agents* from divulging certain confidential information about them to the other party.

What is the mechanism for buyers and sellers to do that? And here is the newest wrinkle:

Designated Agency

Some firms also offer a form of dual agency called "designated agency" where one agent in the firm represents the seller and another represents the buyer. This option (when available) may allow each "designated agent" to more fully represent each party.

What happened to the broker of record being the only agent in an in-house transaction? Now associate licensees are all agents for in-house transactions? We do not think this fits with agency disclosure and the laws of agency. However, this sounds to us exactly like what Texas is doing in the last section of IF THE BROKER ACTS AS AN INTERMEDIARY.
Back to North Carolina:

If you choose the "dual agency" option, remember that since a dual agent's loyalty is divided between two parties with competing interests, it is especially important that you have a clear understanding of * what your relationship is with the *dual agent* and * what the agent will be doing for you in the transaction.

This paragraph is the epitome of divided agency. It does not get any clearer than this.

A dual agent's loyalty is divided between two parties with competing interests, . . .

Just substitute *divided agent's loyalty* for *dual agent's loyalty* and you have the definition of divided agency.

A divided agent's loyalty is divided between two parties with competing interests.

Too Harsh?

For those of you who think we are being too harsh, we have more questions. Are you willing to be accused of participating in a divided agency transaction? Are you willing to disgorge the real estate commission you worked so hard to earn simply because you were trapped in a divided agency situation?

Are you willing to lose your real estate license because of the real estate industry paradigm that makes the Multiple Listing Service protected turf? Are you willing to pay civil fines for being a divided agent? Are you willing to spend time in the gray bar motel?

Solution

One part of the solution to the divided agency minefield is to eliminate the unilateral offer of subagency from the Multiple Listing Service paradigm. A number of years ago, the California Association of Realtors proposed shifting the paradigm of the

Multiple Listing Service to a unilateral offer of compensation. So far, the National Association of Realtors has not endorsed that suggestion.

The other part of the solution to the divided agency minefield is to implement a new working with buyers paradigm. We think by now you know what that would entail. We, as the real estate industry, would have every buyer sign a buyer listing agreement with their real estate agent.

In the next chapter, we will talk about our favorite topic: real estate commissions. Who pays your real estate commission does not determine whom you represent. That may be an odd concept to grasp. Whatever combination you can think of, commission does not determine agency.

Even if the seller pays you a commission as the cooperating agent or the buyer's agent, you can still be representing the buyer exclusively. Even if the buyer pays you a commission, you can be a subagent of the seller. Even if the buyer pays you a commission, you can be representing no one in the transaction.

CHAPTER 12

Commission Does Not Determine Agency

In this chapter, we will talk about our favorite topic: real estate commissions. Who pays your real estate commission does not determine whom you represent. That may be an odd concept to grasp. Whatever combination you can think of, commission does not determine agency.

Think of these possibilities: (1) Even if the seller pays you a commission as the cooperating agent or the buyer's agent, you can still be representing the buyer exclusively; (2) even if the buyer pays you a commission, you can still be a subagent of the seller; or (3) even if the buyer or the seller pays you a commission, you can be representing no one in the transaction.

State Statutes

Every state will have some statutory writing about the possible percentages, rates, or amounts of real estate commissions. California requires the following verbiage under the compensation-to-broker area of the California Association of Realtors buyer broker agreement:

> NOTICE: The amount or rate of real estate commissions is not fixed by law.

What this means is that you can negotiate any compensation package you want with the buyer. It can be a percentage of the purchase price. It can be a percentage of the purchase price and a dollar amount. It can be just a dollar amount. It can be an hourly fee.

Texas requires the following disclosure be given in the Texas Information about Brokerage Service disclosure:

> If you choose to have a broker represent you, you should enter into a written agreement with the broker that clearly establishes the broker's obligations and your obligations. *The agreement should state how and by whom the broker will be paid.* You should have the right to choose the type of representation, if any, you wish to receive. *Your payment of a fee to a broker does not necessarily establish that the broker represents you.* If you have any questions regarding the duties and responsibilities of the broker, you should resolve those questions before proceeding. [Italics added.]

The North Carolina Association of Realtors Working with Real Estate Agents form says the following about real estate commissions:

SELLERS: *Seller's Agent Services and Compensation*

> For representing you and helping you sell your property, you will pay the listing firm a sales commission or fee. The listing agreement must state the amount or method of determining the commission or fee and whether you will allow the firm to share its commission with agents representing the buyer.

BUYERS: *Buyer's Agent Services and Compensation*

> A *buyer's agent* can be compensated in different ways. For example, you can pay the agent out of your own pocket. Or the agent may seek compensation from the seller or listing agent first, but require you to pay if the listing agent refuses. Whatever the case, be sure your

compensation arrangement with your *buyer's agent* is spelled out in a buyer agency agreement before you make an offer to purchase property and that you carefully read and understand the compensation provisions.

Sellers' Agent Working with a Buyer

Seller's agents are compensated by the sellers.

We next have to talk about real estate commissions in a way no one in the real estate industry wants to talk about them. This is the dirty little secret that the real estate industry has spent tens of millions of lobbying dollars to keep under wraps.

Price-Fixed Commissions

We have already established that real estate commissions are not set by law. Yet the perception by the public of the real estate industry paradigm with regard to real estate commissions is that real estate commissions are price-fixed. Where could the public possibly have got that idea?

6 Percent Seller Listing Commission

We as an industry have been charging a 6 percent seller listing commission for 30 to 40 years, depending upon what part of the country you are talking about. The median priced home in California in 1976 sold for $47,000. A seller who paid a real estate broker a 6 percent commission to sell that median priced property would pay $2,820 in real estate commission.

1976 Real Estate Commission

Property Sale Price	$47,000
Commission Percentage	× 6%
Real Estate Commission	$2,820

The median priced home in California in 2006 sold for $470,000. That is a tenfold increase over what the median priced home in California sold for 30 years before.

Tenfold Increase in Median Price

1976 Median Price	$47,000
Tenfold Increase	× 10
2006 Median Price	$470,000

We realize that it would be ludicrous to expect a tenfold reduction in the real estate commission percentage to 0.6 percent to keep the 2006 real estate commission the same $2,820 as it was in 1976. But as the median price has escalated, the 6 percent price-fixed seller real estate commission percentage has remained unchanged.

The 6 percent real estate commission on the 2006 median priced $469,000 California home is $28,140.

2006 Real Estate Commission

Property Sale Price	$469,000
Commission Percentage	× 6%
Real Estate Commission	$28,140

We are all for real estate professionals making money and being paid well for what we do. Like we said at the beginning of this chapter, talking about real estate commissions is our favorite topic. But from an inside or outside the real estate industry point of view, these amounts of real estate commissions might be regarded as excessive.

We feel the best way to be well compensated for services rendered as a real estate professional is to promote consumer choice and healthy competition in our industry. This will transform the conversation of real estate commissions being regarded as excessive in the old paradigm to being regarded as appropriate in the new paradigm.

New Commission Paradigm

We think a new commission model has arrived in the real estate industry. The new paradigm began taking shape about ten years ago. This new commission paradigm has accompanied the proliferation and use of the Internet by real estate buyers.

The Internet

The real estate industry has been changed forever by the Internet. Seventy-seven percent of home buyers used the Internet in 2005 in their search for their next home, according to a National Association of Realtors survey. That compares to only 2 percent of home buyers who used the Internet in 1995 in their search for their next home.

The number of buyers who actually found their next home on the Internet went from less than 1 percent in 1995 to 24 percent in 2005, again according to the National Association of Realtors. According to Rob Snow of E-Trade Mortgage, in some cities, including San Francisco, Cincinnati, and Tampa, more than 30 percent of home sales are generated through the Internet.

We predict that the number of buyers who will find their next home on the Internet will be 35 percent to 40 percent by the time you are reading this book! As Internet listings become more sophisticated, we predict buyers will buy their next home the way they purchase items on eBay or similar Internet auction sites: sight unseen.

National Association of Realtors

David Lereah, chief economist for the National Association of Realtors, was quoted as saying at the National Association of Realtors convention in Orlando, Florida, in November 2004: "More buyers than ever first found their home on the Internet. At the same time, buyers that use the Internet to search are more likely to use a real estate agent"—93 percent of the time. "Contrary to original thought, the Internet didn't destroy our business. The Internet has made the agent more productive because they are able to serve more customers," Mr. Lereah said.

More Sophisticated Buyers

The National Association of Realtors survey also found that buyers are older, with a median age of 39, and more sophisticated than they have been in the past. Buyers are taking the time to do extensive research before making the commitment to a home purchase.

Buyers who used the Internet spent nine weeks looking for their next home. Buyers who did not use the Internet spent only five weeks looking for their next home. However, that does not mean real estate agents were working longer with buyers who used the Internet.

The sophisticated buyers who used the Internet spent the additional four weeks researching the market, viewing Internet home listings, and narrowing their choice of home locations. In some cases, the buyer who used the Internet might spend seven or eight weeks doing research before contacting a real estate agent.

The Old Days

In the old days before the Internet, buyers would look for their next home the old-fashioned way. Buyers would spend hours driving around with you in your car looking at properties. It was usually a very tiring and unproductive experience for both you and the buyer. Looking back, we are amazed that we were able to sell anything!

In our experience, the buyers could not remember the first property we showed them by the time we got to the fifth property of the day. We both made it a rule to show our buyers no more than three properties in a morning or afternoon of driving them around. Otherwise, we were all wasting our time.

Today

Today's sophisticated buyer awakens in the morning to Internet alerts on all the new online listings that have just come on the market. The buyer can check out the pictures, information, and in many cases take a virtual tour of the property.

If the buyer likes what she sees on the Internet, the buyer contacts the real estate agent who has the seller listing and sets an appointment to see the property in person. Then it can be only a matter of hours after receiving the Internet alert that the buyer is having the real estate agent write an offer on the property.

Internet Sites

Homes for sale used to be printed by local Multiple Listing Services in weekly or biweekly book formats. If it was your turn to go to your local Multiple Listing Service to pick up the books for your office, you could wind up getting quite a workout.

These multiple listing books were available only to the real estate agents who subscribed to their local Multiple Listing Services. Now homes for sale are available online to the consumer directly.

Some of these Internet sites include: Realtor.com, which is the official site of the National Association of Realtors; Craigslist.com, which is a giant Internet bulletin board where people sell their stuff, including real estate; Google.com, the giant search engine that comes up with more than 1 million references for real estate.

Zillow.com, which is a site that provides free instant home valuations for more than 70 million homes; Yahoo. com, which provides homes for sale around the country, and HomePages.com, which is a site to find homes, view recently sold homes, and explore neighborhoods.

This is obviously by no means a complete listing of available real estate Internet sites. There are also individual company sites to for-sale-by-owner sites. We presented these six Internet sites as representative of what is out there.

Value of Real State Agent Service May Drop

Real estate agents may find that the value of their service drops as buyers do more legwork of their own on the Internet. In other words, there may be a downward pressure on the amount of real estate commissions consumers are willing to pay. "The full impact of the Internet has not been realized, primarily because business has been going up each year," said Steve Murray, editor of the trade magazine *Real Trends* in Littleton, Colorado.

Murray's data show that the average commission paid to real estate agents dropped from 6.1 percent of a home's price in 1991 to 5.1 percent in 2003, the most recent statistics available. Murray attributes this to the increase in the number of agents competing for the available real estate business during this time period.

The competition has only got more intense in the go-go real estate markets of 2004, 2005, and 2006. There have been 7.5 million to 8 million new and existing home sales each year during these three years.

At the peak, there were 1.5 million residential real estate agents who were members of the National Association of Realtors. Without taking into account the number of real estate licensees who were not members of the National Association of Realtors, this is about five sales annually per real estate agent.

Sales per Agent Annually

Number of Sales	7,500,000
Number of Agents	1,500,000

$7,500,000 / 1,500,000 = 5$ Sales

Murray expects that in a normal market the use of the Internet will be among the factors that will drive real estate commissions down. "We don't see any particular stopping point," he said.

Discount Brokers

To be fair, the new commission paradigm includes so-called discount seller listing brokers. For those sellers who want to do more of the job of selling their property, there is a corresponding lowering of the full-service 6 percent real estate commission.

We have seen this lowering of real estate commissions go from 6 percent to 5 percent to 4 percent to 3 percent to 2 percent to 1 percent to a flat fee, depending on the menu of services the seller wants the real estate agent to perform. Obviously, this puts downward pressure on the overall real estate commission percentage for the total number of real estate transactions handled by real estate licensees.

Let's take a look at one such menu of services. This is from a company called Estate Realty located in Dallas, Texas. They have a web site called LeasetoBuy.com. Although the lease-to-buy program is directed at buyers, the web site includes a menu of services the company offers to sellers.

This menu of services is called by the company Service Options. We think this is smart marketing and very consumer friendly. It also addresses the Federal Trade Commission (FTC) complaint regarding illegally restraining competition that we have talked about with the FTC's action against the Austin Board of Realtors in 2006.

What we find especially interesting is that the second service the company will provide to its seller clients after a market analysis is Internet exposure. Internet exposure is offered no matter which service option the seller chooses. The company will put three of the seller's favorite pictures and a paragraph or two of the seller's description of the property on the Internet.

Three Commission Percentages

There are three commission percentages that are offered, based on the service options the company provides. The 6 percent commission is the premium account. This corresponds to the typical full-service brokerage exclusive authorization and right-to-sell listing available throughout the real estate industry.

The 4 percent commission is an exclusive agency agreement. The seller reserves the right to sell the property themselves but agrees to pay a 4 percent commission if the company brings a buyer at a price the seller agrees to sell for.

This option requires the seller pay a nonrefundable $495 fee at the time of signing the seller listing agreement and hold all the open houses. The fee is credited toward the real estate commission at the time of closing if a broker sells the property.

Seller Protected

Under this option, the company agrees to protect the seller. "Keep in mind that we agree to represent you and pay other brokers 3% if they get a buyer. This commission is no different to a buyer's broker so you should not fear that you will be shunned and qualified buyers taken to the competition."

This is smart marketing and new commission paradigm thinking all in one. This real estate company will take a 1 percent seller listing commission if another real estate company brings an acceptable buyer. Of course, if the seller listing company brings an acceptable buyer, the seller listing company will receive the entire 4 percent real estate commission.

Buyer Broker

The 3 percent commission is the buyer broker plan. Again, we like the smart marketing and new commission strategy. The company will do a market analysis and give the property Internet exposure. Yet the company will be exclusively representing the buyer in the transaction!

"Our 3% listing is a commitment from you to us that you will pay us a 3% commission if we bring you an acceptable buyer. You are on your own with this program. All the buyers we introduce to your home will be represented by us. If saving money is your plan and you like to be in complete control, this plan will get you quality exposure for maybe nothing."

We think this is brilliant. You have a written commitment from a seller, who is really a for sale by owner, to pay you a 3 percent real estate commission. Yet you have no agency relationship or fiduciary duties to the seller. Remember, we said in the new real estate commission paradigm, commission does not determine agency!

Attorneys

The ultimate discount brokers are attorneys who are realtors. We have already touched on the fact that attorneys are just itching to jump into the real estate business beyond the closing side to the buying and selling side.

Here is an ad in our local Dallas newspaper we found as we were writing this book. We think it represents a growing trend in the real estate industry. We like competition.

1% Commission!

Call Jim 815-555-1222
Sell with Attorney/Realtor

Show Us the Money

We are going to wrap up our conversation about the new real estate commission paradigm with some thoughts about being paid like a professional. We will also show you some calculations to stimulate how you think about the time you spend in the real estate industry.

9 A.M. to 5 P.M., *Monday through Friday*

Just about every professional you do business with keeps what we would call regular hours. We invite you to think about keeping regular hours in your real estate business. This may be the hardest thing we have asked you to think about so far.

The real estate industry paradigm for time is perhaps harder to shift than the real estate industry paradigm for any other area. We are told when we get in the business that we are in business for ourselves. We are told we are entrepreneurs.

Some of us have worked 60-hour weeks, 70-hour weeks, or even 80-hour weeks in our real estate business. Some of us have worked even more than 80-hour weeks. You know who you are.

Some of us have worked 30 days in a row, 60 days in a row, or even 90 days in a row in our real estate business. Some of us have worked even more than 90 days in a row. And you know who you are.

We have a question for you. Do you work so much to make more money? If you answered yes, we have another question for you. If you could make the same amount of money working less time, would you be interested? All of you are answering yes.

Some of you are thinking that if you could work less time and make the same amount of money then you would like to work the same amount of time and make even more money! You know who you are.

Calculations

Let's do some calculations. Professionals who work 50 weeks per year (with two weeks of vacation) for 40 hours per week work 2,000 hours in the course of a year. We will call that a standard professional year. We are talking about attorneys, judges, accountants, doctors, dentists, architects. Anyway, you get the picture.

Standard Professional Year

50 Weeks
× 40 Hours
──────────
2,000 Hours

Professionals who work 50 weeks per year (with two weeks of vacation) for 60 hours per week work 3,000 hours in the course of a year. We will call that an extended professional year.

Extended Professional Year

50 Weeks
× 60 Hours
──────────
3,000 Hours

Make Money with Your Real Estate License

How much money do you want to make in a year as a real estate professional? Do you want to make $50,000, $100,000, $200,000 or _____? Let's say you want to make $100,000 per year. We want to give you a way to think about it like other professionals think about it.

Attorney

An attorney who wants to make $100,000 per year would think about it this way. How many billable hours would I have to work if I was paid so much an hour? If the attorney was paid $50 per hour, the attorney would have to work 2,000 billable hours in one year to make $100,000.

$100,000 Yearly

2,000 Hours
× $50/Hour
──────────
$100,000 Yearly

Real Estate Agent

So you would have to work only 2,000 hours in the course of a year and average $50 per hour to make $100,000. What if you could average $100 per hour for the standard professional year of 2,000 hours worked? Then you would make $200,000.

Standard Professional Year

2,000 Hours
× $100/Hour
$200,000 Yearly

So what are you worth per hour as a real estate professional? If you want to make $100,000 per year and you have trouble with the idea of being paid $50 per hour, find a number you are comfortable with.

Let's say you are comfortable making $35 per hour. Now instead of working 2,000 hours in a year to make $100,000, you must work almost 3,000 hours in a year to make $100,000.

$100,000 Yearly

2,857 Hours
× $35/Hour
$100,000 Yearly

This averages working more than 57 hours per week for 50 weeks.

2,857 Hours per Year / 50 Weeks = 57.14 Hours per Week

Extended Professional Year

Some of you are going to work the extended professional year of 3,000 hours. Some of you will be quite comfortable making $50 per hour or even $100 per hour. That will have you being paid quite handsomely as a real estate professional working in the new real estate commission paradigm.

Extended Professional Year at $50/Hour

3,000 Hours
× $50/Hour
$150,000 Yearly

Extended Professional Year at $100/Hour

3,000 Hours
× $100/Hour
$300,000 Yearly

Our Point

We reiterate our point that in the old working with buyers paradigm you do not feel one pang of guilt making a $15,000 commission selling a buyer a $500,000 property. This is receiving the standard 3 percent commission to the selling office that brings the buyer.

Why should you feel guilty in the new working with buyers paradigm making $100 per hour? You would have to work 150 hours at $100 an hour, which is almost four 40-hour work weeks (160 hours) or two and a half 60-hour work weeks (150 hours), to make a $15,000 commission.

$15,000 Commission

150 Hours
× $100/Hour
$15,000 Commission

Who is ready to get paid like other professionals? Who is ready to benefit from the new real estate commission paradigm? If you answered "I am" to both of these questions, then you are ready to hear the next question. Who is ready to be a buyer's agent?

If you answered "I am" to this question, you are ready for the next chapter. Being a buyer's agent means you need to think, talk, and act like a buyer's agent. Let's double your real estate commissions working with buyers.

CHAPTER 13

Being a Buyer's Agent

In this chapter, we will teach you how to *be* a buyer's agent. We will coach you how to think, talk, and act like a buyer's agent. By embracing the new buyers paradigm you will be on your way to being a true buyer's agent.

You will actually have to walk the walk and talk the talk to be successful. Our definition of you being a successful buyer's agent is doubling your commissions working with buyers in the next 12 months. We are sure you are all interested in that outcome.

We also want you to be comfortable being a buyer's agent. This starts with you being comfortable with yourself. Once you are comfortable with yourself, it leads to the buyer being comfortable with you. Not surprisingly, this also has the seller's agent and the seller being comfortable with you as a buyer's agent.

Thinking Like a Buyer's Agent

How does a buyer's agent think? To begin to formulate the answer to this question, you have to first put yourself in the buyer's shoes. What does a buyer think about during the process of buying real estate? What motivates a buyer to buy their next home? To understand this, you must literally become a student of human behavior.

Thinking like a buyer's agent starts even before you say your first word to a buyer. You actually have to think about being a buyer's agent not only before you even open your

159

mouth but before you take any actions at all. In fact, at this point in time, it really does not matter what you think . . . just yet. We should start first with understanding how the buyer thinks.

How Does the Buyer Think?

First, there are some motivating factors that cause the buyer to think about leaving their current home. Their current home is too big or too small. The current home is too expensive or not expensive enough. The current home is in the suburbs and the buyer wants to live downtown. The current home is downtown and the buyer wants to live in the country.

Other motivating factors might include the buyer being transferred to another city. The buyer is retiring. The kids are starting school. The kids are going to college. The kids are coming back to live at home. Elderly parents are moving in. There has been a divorce, illness, or death in the family.

Understand the Motivating Factors

Your job as the buyer's agent begins with you understanding the motivating factors that are having the buyer seriously consider buying another home. Sometimes, one motivating factor is enough to have a buyer want to move. Sometimes, it is a combination of several motivating factors. How does the buyer take that first step to buy another home?

Overcome Habit Patterns

The first step the buyer takes to actually buy another home is to have the motivating factors overcome habit patterns. No matter how much better life could be in the next home or how inconvenient life is in the current home, people stick with what is familiar to them.

This can make habit patterns hard to break. We have found that we can help buyers break their habit patterns by getting them excited about buying their next home. Then the excitement of buying their next home becomes an important motivating factor.

Generate Excitement

The motivating factors that have a buyer contemplate moving must generate a level of excitement in the buyer. This is a level of excitement at the prospect of living in their next home that will overcome all obstacles. One of your jobs as the buyer's agent is to have the buyer stay in touch with that excitement throughout the home-buying process. But beware of the demotivating factors.

Understand the Demotivating Factors

Your job as the buyer's agent also makes it necessary for you to understand the demotivating factors that will have the buyer seriously considering *not* buying another home. Sometimes, one demotivating factor is enough to have a buyer want to back out of a deal. Sometimes, it is a combination of several demotivating factors.

We have had buyers be demotivated about buying their perfect home because of the color of the exterior paint! We know how dumb this sounds. We are thinking, "Are these people crazy?" But remember, we said you must become a student of human behavior.

Become a Student of Human Behavior

Real estate buyers come in all types of thinking shapes and sizes. Sometimes, you can use logic to get your buyer back on track. Sometimes, you can use common sense. Other times, we have found we just have to say nothing but rather listen to what our buyers say to understand what they think.

Our first inclination with our demotivated-because-of-the-exterior-color buyers was to laugh. Our second inclination, as we have already said, was thinking, "Are these people crazy?" Our third inclination was to inform them that all they needed to do was paint the exterior of their new home a color that they liked.

We did none of these things. We just listened as the husband and wife buyers had a conversation about the paint after we had completed looking at the property. After all, they had not asked us our thoughts on the matter.

Although Bill's tendency was to fix the problem, he was smart enough to look over at Chantal before he opened his mouth. Chantal shook her head, indicating that Bill should say nothing. We just continued to listen to our buyers talk.

Phobia 1

It turns out the wife had a phobia associated with the blue color of the home's exterior paint. In the course of their conversation, the husband suggested repainting the exterior. This was the obvious solution, right? Bill had thought of that.

The twist was would the wife be okay knowing the blue paint was still attached to the house if it was just covered over by the new paint color? The wife told her husband she would not be okay with that! The husband then suggested that all the blue paint be scraped off before a new color was added.

That solution worked for the wife. The husband turned toward us and asked if we knew a good painter who would be meticulous in removing the blue paint. Now we had something useful to say to our buyers. We told them yes, we knew the perfect painter for the job.

We wrote an offer that was accepted. The rest of the transaction ran like clockwork. We closed escrow. We contacted our painter, who removed all the offending blue paint. The new paint was applied, and the buyers moved in.

We learned to trust our buyers from this transaction. We had a buyer listing agreement in place. We knew that if they did not buy a particular property for any reason, we could find them another property. We realized being a buyer's agent meant that we had to respect our buyer's way of thinking, even if it did not make sense to our way of thinking.

This is so crucial to your success we are going to restate it: Realize being a buyer's agent means that you have to respect your buyer's way of thinking even if it does not make sense to your way of thinking.

Phobia 2

We had buyers that wanted to back out of a deal because they thought the new home that we found them was too good to be true! The buyer's thinking was something along the lines of "There has got to be something wrong with this deal" because everything was going so smoothly.

We had looked at the home. We made an offer that was accepted by the seller. We were moving through the closing process. The buyers were thrilled at first. Then buyer's remorse set in. But it was a different kind of buyer's remorse than we were used to.

The buyers became convinced that the combination of us finding them the perfect next home coupled with us getting them the exact price and terms they wanted was not possible. There had to be something wrong somewhere in this transaction.

Their excitement about living in their new home was being overcome by the twin demotivating factors of (1) getting what they wanted was not possible and (2) there had to be something wrong. The buyers were literally waiting with trepidation for the proverbially shoe to drop.

Our job was to understand the buyers' twin demotivating factors and get them back in touch with their excitement. We realized that if we could introduce something being wrong into the transaction then this would actually alleviate the waiting-with-trepidation, something-had-to-be-wrong phobia.

We did not have to look too far. As with most real estate transactions, there are usually one or more little problems that come up in the course of the closing. Sure enough, the preliminary title report indicated a judgment lien against the seller's title to the property. This would have to be cleared for the deal to go through.

This was no big deal. We knew that, the seller knew that, the seller's real estate agent knew that, the title company knew that, the escrow knew that, and the buyers' lender knew that. The title would be cleared and the lien paid from the seller's proceeds in the closing.

We made a big deal of it, however, when we met with the buyers to go over the preliminary title report. We told them we had some bad news. The preliminary title report indicated a judgment lien against the seller's title. If we could not get the judgment lien cleared from the title, we would not be able to close the deal.

We could literally feel relief exude from the buyers when we told them the "bad news." The buyers knowingly looked at each other and talked about how they both knew something bad was going to happen. The deal was just too good to be true.

We nodded in agreement with the buyer. Then a strange thing happened. The buyers asked us what options we could come up with to solve the title problem. They were really excited about getting this property and did not want to lose it. They told us if we could solve this problem and get them this property, they would be forever grateful to us.

Once the buyers were told about a "problem" they knew was going to come up, they were able to deal with that known situation. What was driving them crazy was having to deal with the unknown "problem" they were sure was going to happen. We made them feel right about the fact that they knew there was going to be a "problem."

In a sense, we did the opposite of a takeaway in this situation. We did an add-to by making a bigger deal out of the preliminary title report than was merited. But we knew our buyers. They needed us to make a big deal of something in the transaction in order to feel comfortable.

The title was cleared, and the deal closed. Our buyers thought we were fantastic because we solved the title problem. By the way, we told them after the closing about our little charade. We do not think it even registered with them. In their minds, the judgment lien was a big problem they knew was going to happen. We did not think it was our job to disabuse them of their way of thinking.

Now that you understand how a buyer thinks and what a buyer thinks about, it's time to learn about buyer's agent thinking.

So Exactly What Does the Buyer's Agent Think?

The buyer's agent is constantly thinking about the best ways to represent the buyer. Like we said earlier, thinking like a buyer's agent starts even before you say your first word to a buyer.

You actually have to think about being a buyer's agent not only before you even open your mouth but also before you take any action at all. You have to prepare yourself to think as a buyer's agent.

We started this process with understanding how a buyer thinks and what a buyer thinks about. We learned that how a buyer thinks and what they think about can appear strange to your way of thinking. So what is next?

Preparing Yourself to Think

Education and information are always the keys to ways of thinking. You have already educated yourself on a new real estate paradigm. You understand buyers in general. You now must purposefully set the paradigms, or thinking perspectives, in your mind.

Make it your own. Adapt it to your personality. Be true to your chosen way of thinking. Do this by being sure to view everything about your thinking, speaking, actions, and entire way of being through your chosen paradigm.

Whatever measures up to your required standards, keep it! If something does not measure up, throw it away! You have now run your mental checklist of your standards and know what stays and what goes. Now it is time to solidify your way of being. This takes action on your part.

Taking Action

The first thing to do is write your mental checklist. On one side, write what you are keeping. On the other side, write what you are tossing. This way, you start to truly register in your mind your chosen successful way of being as well as your reminders of what no longer fits your successful way of being.

Self-Talk, Practice, and Mirror Work

We highly recommend self-talk, practice, and mirror work. What we mean by self-talk is for you to have an internal dialogue that pumps you up. Your self-talk could be labeled as positive mental attitude, meditation, prayer, aliveness, a pep talk, good self-image, or five or ten other things.

Our point is that your self-talk should be building you up to be a successful buyer's agent. If your self-talk is negative or depressing you, write it on your mental checklist side of what you are tossing and then toss it. Maintain this by practicing positive self-talk daily!

Another thing to practice is your buyer listing presentation before you are in front of a real client. We are not recommending you go for slick or snazzy in your presentation. We want you to know the flow of the presentation.

We want you to feel comfortable with the material. And most importantly, we want you to be yourself. That is why we think it is critical to do your buyer listing presentation in the mirror.

Some of you may already do mirror work. Congratulations, we already know that you are successful in your real estate business. For those of you whose mirror work is limited to putting on makeup or shaving in the morning, we are talking to you.

We know it may be uncomfortable to be looking at the person in the mirror that is staring back at you while you are doing your presentation. If you are uncomfortable with the person in the mirror, think how uncomfortable the client will be!

Mirror work is designed to have you *be* with the person in the mirror. It helps you get over the discomfort, nervousness, embarrassment, and so forth with the person in the mirror. The goal is for you is to be comfortable, calm, and self-confident in front of the client.

Time Management

As a buyer's agent, you are always thinking about what is the best use of the buyer's time. This in turn has you make the best use of your own time. You study the buyer's needs and parameters enough to know the best way to support fulfilling your buyer's needs with the minimum amount of time expended.

This is the key to what makes you really worth the compensation the buyer has agreed to pay you. You are going to maximize the buyer's time as well as your own time. This will increase your income and increase your effectiveness.

Obtain a Commitment from the Buyer

The only way you can deliver on making the best use of the buyer's time is for you to obtain a commitment from the buyer. This is why we say it is so important to make a buyer's listing presentation. Once the buyer makes the commitment to retain you as their buyer's agent, you have something solid to keep the buyer's excitement alive.

Even if you find the buyers the perfect next home, 9 times out of 10 buyers with no commitment to buy will not buy that perfect home. We say it this way: The likelihood of you having a buyer purchase a home without a commitment to buy is the same as the likelihood of you being able to nail Jell-O to the wall.

Handle Buyer's Remorse

Another thing you have to think about as a buyer's agent is handling buyer's remorse. We have found that it is never a question of *if* the buyer will experience buyer's remorse. It is always a question of *when* the buyer will experience buyer's remorse.

We have included buyer's remorse under time management for a reason. By thinking ahead about what you are going to say and what actions you are going to take when buyer's remorse rears its ugly head, you can direct the buyer back on track in a timely manner.

Directing the buyer back on track involves having them look at what the buyer said is their commitment. That is another reason why having a commitment from the buyer in the form of a buyer's listing agreement is so important. Before you can make a great presentation to get an agreement, however, you must first be sure you talk like a professional buyer's agent.

Talking Like a Buyer's Agent

Talking like a buyer's agent starts with the first words you say to a potential buyer in setting up your initial appointment. Talking like a buyer's agent then moves through the stages of the buyer listing presentation, the offer presentation, the closing, and the after-closing follow-up.

We are going to focus here on setting up the initial appointment. You certainly get to demonstrate your ability to talk like a buyer's agent at the buyer listing presentation, the offer presentation, the closing, and the after-closing follow-up. Here we are concerned about *being* a buyer's agent and talking like a buyer's agent from the beginning.

Setting Up the Initial Appointment

In today's world, there are three ways to set up an initial appointment with a client. The first way is when you are in a face-to-face conversation. The second way is when you are speaking on the telephone. The third way is when you are in an e-mail or text message environment.

A possible fourth way is to have a third party set up the appointment without any face-to-face meeting or communication between you and the client. We call this the blind date meeting. We do not recommend it. Remember, we are in the people business.

Although e-mailing and text messaging are becoming a more and more prevalent means of communication, we think these mediums are much better utilized after you have already established a relationship with the client. And although it is possible to have a face-to-face meeting to establish an actual buyer listing presentation appointment, we are going to focus on what to say to the client on the telephone.

Telephone Conversation

One of two things will generate a telephone conversation between you and the client. The client will call you or you will call the client. The client will be calling you on an ad call, which is really a cold call, or because of a referral. You will be calling the client as a cold call or a referral.

The purpose of the telephone conversation with the client, whether it is on a cold or a referral call, is to set a buyer listing appointment. We support the old adage that you can not sell the client either their next home or yourself over the phone. We support this adage up to a point.

You obviously have to sell yourself to the client in the sense that the client agrees to set an appointment to meet with you. If the client is turned off by you in the phone conversation, there is no way the client will agree to a face-to-face meeting.

Caveat

We want to give you a word of warning here. As you are making the transition from the old buyers paradigm to the new buyers paradigm, client ad calls will test you being a buyer's agent. Remember, we have said that the old paradigm has trained buyers to call on an ad, want to meet you immediately at your office to go look at the property, or just meet you at the property.

When you are being a buyer's agent, you will refuse to do business in this manner. The temptation will be that the buyer will suck you into operating from the old paradigm over the phone! The buyer will tell you they have to buy something today. If you want to make a commission, you had better jump up and meet them at the property.

Do not take the bait. Yes, it is possible that the buyer is legitimate and will be buying their next home today. If you refuse to meet them at the property, the buyer will just call another real estate agent and write the offer through them. The other agent will receive the commission you would have received. But what are the chances of that actually happening? We think the possibility of this happening is one time in a thousand chances.

How about you being able to handle the ad call in a professional manner? You are the one who should be in control of the call. You are the one who should be enrolling the client in you being a buyer's agent. Let's see how to do that.

Cold Call

Let's start with what you are going to say on a cold call with a client calling on a seller-listing ad. We think this will be the vast majority of cold calls that most of you will be involved with. We are going to assume that the call to your office has been answered by the receptionist and is being transferred to your desk.

First though, for those of you who are proficient at outbound cold calling, we salute you and recommend you keep on saying what you are saying. As long as you are generating appointments with clients, your cold calling is a success. Now to the incoming cold call.

Cold Call Script

Hello! My name is _____. Thank you for calling. To whom am I speaking? Listen to the response and write down the name.

Where did you hear about the property you are calling about? Listen to the response and write down the answer.

What particularly interested you about our ad? Listen to the response and write down the pertinent information.

That property is located in the _____ section of _____ city. Where do you live? Listen to the response and write down the answer.

That property has ___ bedrooms, ___ bathrooms, and about ___ square feet of living space. **Do you own a home now?** Listen to the response and write down the answer.

This home also has the following features (list important features): _____

_____

_____, and

_____.

Are you looking for a home like this? Listen to the response and write down the answer. Whether or not the client is interested in the home they called about is irrelevant. The client is interested in some next home that you are going to sell them.

_____ (Use client's name), **I am so glad you called. I can help you find your perfect next home. I am a buyer's agent and can show you any home on the market, including new homes and for-sale-by-owner homes.**

I suggest setting up an appointment so I can learn exactly what you want in your next home. Can you come in now or would Tuesday evening or Wednesday evening be better for you?

That is how you handle an incoming cold call. Remember to keep your own personality in the script. Now, what do you do with a referral?

Referral Call

Referral calls are a much easier row to hoe. One of your former clients, a friend, or a family member has sung your praises. You are already speaking into what we would call a warm listening. Let's have you making the referral call to the client.

Referral Call Script

Hello! My name is _____. I am from ABC Realty. To whom am I speaking? Listen to the response and write down the name. If this is not the person you have been referred to, ask to speak to that person.

May I please speak to _____? (The name of the client.) Once you are speaking to the client say:

_____ (Use client's name)**, I have been given your name and number by** _____ (The name of the person who referred you). _____ (Use the name of the person who referred you) **said you are thinking about buying your next home. How exciting! Do you have a few minutes to talk?** Listen to the response. If the answer is yes, proceed. If the answer is no, say:

_____ (Use client's name)**, would tonight at 7 o'clock or tomorrow night at 8 o'clock be better for you?** Listen to the response and write down the information. Call back at the agreed upon time. Let's pick up the conversation.

_____ (Use client's name.)**, I am so glad** _____ (The name of the person who referred you) **told you about me. I can help you find your perfect next home. I am a buyer's agent and can show you any home on the market, including new homes and for-sale-by-owner homes.**

I suggest setting up an appointment so I can learn exactly what you want in your next home. Would Tuesday evening or Wednesday evening be better for you?

Now that you have an appointment as a buyer's agent, you must always remember to act like a buyer's agent.

Acting Like a Buyer's Agent

Acting like a buyer's agent starts with being a true representative of the buyer. You are acting like a buyer's agent when you are being a fiduciary of the buyer. The best part of being a buyer's agent is knowing that when you have a buyer listing agreement with a buyer in a real estate transaction you actually control the real estate transaction.

Obviously, acting like a buyer's agent starts from the initial appointment-setting conversation you have with the buyer and goes all the way through the closing of the transaction. Our focus here will be on the offer presentation. This is where acting like a buyer's agent can have the most impact for the buyer. What occurs at the offer presentation determines whether the buyer gets a good deal.

The Offer Presentation

In the old paradigm, we have referred to the table where the offer is presented as the conspiracy table. In residential real estate transactions, this table is usually the seller's kitchen table. The seller is present. The seller's listing agent is present. The agent presenting the buyer's offer is present. The only person not present is the buyer!

This can lend itself to the people present at the table intentionally or unintentionally putting together a counter-offer for a higher price than the buyer offered. The buyer is left unsure if the agent who presented their offer acted in the buyer's best interest.

Did the agent who presented the buyer's offer fight for the offer? Did the agent sell the benefits of the offer to the seller and the seller's agent? Or did the agent give away that the buyer really likes the property and would probably pay more than the buyer's original offer?

New Paradigm

In the new paradigm, by acting like the buyer's agent you avoid the trap of the conspiracy table. It may still be just the seller, the seller's agent, and you, as the buyer's agent, at the table. However, you are truly negotiating the transaction. If at first you don't succeed, present another offer.

Because you have a binding commitment with the buyer through the buyer listing agreement, if the deal falls through you can go find another property. You don't lose the buyer. In fact acting like a buyer's agent, you will knock a deal out if that is what is best for the buyer.

In the next chapter, we will talk about buyer loyalty. By thinking, talking, and acting like a buyer's agent, you generate buyer loyalty. Because loyalty is a two-way street, by being a buyer's agent you make it easy for your buyer to trust and believe in you.

Buyer Loyalty

B uyer loyalty is one of the outcomes of the new buyers paradigm. Without buyer loyalty, you have the old buyers paradigm. There is no buyer loyalty possible in that old way of thinking. In that paradigm, buyers can typically behave only as, in old insider industry terms, liars, flakes, and lookie-loos.

In the new way of thinking, buyers are honest, committed, and loyal. *Loyal* is defined as "constant and faithful in any relation or obligation implying trust or confidence." *Loyalty* is defined as "the state, quality, or fact of being loyal; fidelity, allegiance." The definitions of *loyal* and *loyalty* contain components that sound to us very similar to components in the definition of *fiduciary*.

We have already established that when you are a buyer's agent you are a fiduciary of the buyer. You have an obligation of allegiance and trust as a fiduciary or agent of the buyer. In other words, you are loyal to the buyer.

The buyer is the principal, and you are the agent. The buyer is not your fiduciary. However, the buyer who is loyal to you is faithful and constant in their relationship to you as their agent. The buyer who is loyal to you also has an obligation of allegiance to and trust in you.

Loyalty is a two-way street. Your buyers are loyal to you because they trust you to do the best possible job for them. You are loyal to your buyers because you trust they will adhere to the buyer listing agreement they made with you. Loyalty is real because of the buyer listing agreement. There is no pressure from you on the buyer to buy anything less than exactly what fits their needs.

Your Job as a Fiduciary

Your job as a fiduciary of the buyer is to locate the appropriate property for the buyer. After you have located the appropriate property, your job is to negotiate the best price and terms possible for your buyer. You complete your job by making sure everything is finished in a timely manner during the closing or escrow process. Let's start with locating appropriate properties. How will you begin?

Locating the Appropriate Property

There are two important aspects to locating the appropriate property for your buyer. You must first know all your buyer's property parameters, requirements, and needs. Second, you must make a timely property search.

Buyer Parameters, Requirements, and Needs

We have talked about writing the buyer's property requirements on the buyer listing agreement. Remember, as part of your fiduciary loyalty to the buyer, you agree to give the buyer the first right of refusal to make an offer on property you locate that fits their parameters in the process of your search.

Once you know what the buyer wants, you can start your search for the perfect property with the best deal for the buyer. These are deals that you have agreed to find for your buyer(s). Besides using all your resources to find them a great deal, you also have to be able to separate the good deals from the bad to do the best job for your buyer. Using all your resources to find a great deal and knowing the difference are the two areas the buyer will be especially counting on you.

The Search

Now that you know what you are looking for, you can start your search for the perfect property with the best deal for your buyer. There are several general areas in which you can start your search. You can check out your company listings, Multiple Listing Service listings, and, last but not least the largest area to look, the open market.

The Open Market

There are more properties on the open market than there are listed with brokers. Properties are everywhere! Nothing is unavailable to you now that you have a loyal and committed buyer. You can do whatever you need to do to find the best property and the best deal for your buyer.

You will never again waste your time looking for property. You can even tell your buyer that they can bring you whatever properties they may find as well because you can now help them with any property anywhere.

Feel free to look everywhere for property. Start somewhere simple. Start with the classifieds, both print and Internet. There are 13 key words or phrases to look for that may help you find a great deal for your buyer.

13 Key Words or Phrases

1. Must Sell—Anytime you encounter the phrase *must sell,* you may have come upon the property owner able to give your buyer a great deal.

We have heard some pretty strange reasons for selling as well as the fairly standard, legitimate reasons for selling.

You may discover that they are selling because they are behind on their mortgage payments. You may discover they are selling because they have lost their job. Whatever the property owner's must-sell reason is gives you an opportunity to make a good deal for your buyer.

2. Under Market—This is another property to get a great deal for your buyer. Of course, you have to investigate to determine if the property owner really knows what they are talking about. *Under market* to the property owner may still be overpriced to your buyer. Knowing value is critical to your

success in any real estate transaction, especially when you are in a fiduciary position.

3. Below Appraisal—This is a phrase we like to hear. Sounds like this may be an obvious good deal for our buyer. But you have to be careful here. Below what appraised value? Are we talking below the appraised value for insurance purposes?

Are we talking about the appraised value for property tax purposes? Are we talking about below the appraised value for a home equity loan? Or are we talking about below the appraised value for a recent market comparison? The last value is the only one that counts.

4. Transferred—*Transferred* can mean *transferred*. Or *transferred* can be a code word for a property owner in distress. In today's economy, when someone is transferred, they are often happy to have a job to be transferred to. But they may have been out of a job for a while and be in pre-foreclosure. You may be able to put together a great deal for your buyer.

5. Divorce—When you see or hear the word *divorce,* there is often a real estate deal close by. Statistics tell us that most real estate in a divorce winds up being sold so that the assets can be divided between the ex-spouses. We have found the best offers in a divorce-involved property are all-cash offers. Each side is willing to take a hit on the purchase price because each wants as much of their equity as possible in cash. This could make for a good deal for your buyer.

6. Lost Job/Laid Off—As a real estate agent looking for a good deal for your buyer, when you see *lost job* or *laid off* in a real estate ad or when one of your personal contacts gives you an alert about someone losing a job, more than likely there is a real estate deal to be made. It is a fact that most people live paycheck to paycheck. When they lose the paycheck, the family home may not be far behind.

7. Illness/Accident Ad—Unfortunately, illnesses and accidents are a fact of life. Sometimes, your job as a real estate agent can really help people out of a tough situation while getting your buyer a great deal. A real estate ad we saw read something like this:

Accident forces sale.
3Br/2Ba 2-story family home.
Only $325,000.
817-555-2455

    We called and found out that the owner had been in a serious car accident. They had a two-story home and could no longer climb the stairs. They were selling because they needed a one-story home and money for medical bills. This was a good deal looking for a taker. That would be you with your buyer.

    8. Death—"Death forces sale." This was the heading of a classified ad we read one morning in our local newspaper. This was a pretty tough situation. But the widow needed to sell because her husband had died after suffering a heart attack. A foreclosure notice of default had already been posted. This was another opportunity for a buyer's good deal.

    9. Owner Will Carry—When you see or hear *owner will carry,* you have found a built-in real estate lender to finance the deal. The property owner is going to act as the lender. They are going to carry a mortgage or trust deed for a portion of or for the entire purchase price. We have found that a property owner in distress will offer to carry financing in order to make their property more attractive to more buyers. If the property is right for your buyers, then go for it!

    10. Nothing Down—No down payment. *Nothing down* means a property owner wants their property to be the most competitive one on the market. This can also be an indication that the property owner does not have a lot of time because of an impending foreclosure. The property owner may just want someone to take over their loan payments and get on down the road. Of course, *nothing down* may just mean nothing down and you still may be able to make a good deal for your buyer because of the great terms.

    11. 100 Percent Financing—A variation of nothing down is *100 percent financing.* We may have a distressed property owner who has to sell the property and is willing to finance the sale rather than lose all their equity. This is one of those phrases that we never pass up when we encounter it. One thing to

look out for when you see *100 percent financing* is a property that will go with Veterans Administration (VA) financing. This means the property owner will cooperate with a VA buyer. Although there is no down payment for the VA buyer, this is not seller financing that you can use with all real estate buyers.

12. Motivated Seller—A *motivated seller* is a motivated property owner. As a real estate agent looking for a good deal for your buyer, you are looking for motivated sellers. Property owners in preforeclosure are motivated sellers. A motivated seller might just give your buyer the deed to their property and walk away!

It would be fair to say that all the property owners with whom we have done business in the foreclosure arena are motivated. When we encounter a property owner who is not motivated, we usually have a very hard time doing business with them. Don't waste your time or your buyer's time.

13. Foreclosure Ad—Usually, you see something like this in a real estate classified ad:

Losing home to foreclosure.
Make offer.
4Br/2Ba $273,500
3 years old.
682-555-2455

Call on the ad. Identify yourself as a real estate agent with a committed qualified buyer. Find out when the foreclosure sale is scheduled to occur. Set an appointment to meet with the property owner. If they have equity in the property, suggest to the buyer an offer to buy the equity. If they have little or no equity in the property, suggest to your buyer to make a short-sale offer.

Foreclosures are a huge source of possible good deals for your buyer. There are two ways to search the public record to glean information about foreclosures or potential foreclosures. You can do it yourself. Or you can pay a foreclosure service to provide you with the foreclosure information.

Personal Contacts

Enlisting the help of personal contacts is a great way to find a good deal for your buyer. Tell your family and friends you have qualified real estate buyers. Let people know at church and at social groups that you are a real estate agent with qualified buyers. You may learn of an impending divorce. You may hear about an illness. Someone may have recently died in an accident. You may hear about an upcoming plant closing. There is the gossip of a scandal at city hall. You just may be able to find that perfect deal for your committed buyer.

Scouting

Doing your own scouting is always a great way to find a good deal for your buyer. Driving your buyer's target area a different way each day can lead you to a good deal. Use side streets rather than thoroughfares. Take an extra fifteen minutes driving home from work to look at property. Shop at a different grocery store. Drive through unfamiliar neighborhoods.

Tell your buyer to feel free to do it, too, if they feel inclined. This frees them up to do what they will anyway and opens the door to them bringing you the information as part of their commitment.

Look at bulletin boards in stores and Laundromats for real estate for sale ads. Talk to people you do business with, like the dry cleaner, shoe repair, cable guy, and plumber, and let them know you are a real estate agent with qualified buyers looking for property.

Open Houses

Visiting open houses is another way to find your buyer a good deal. Make it a point to drive around your buyer's target area on Saturday or Sunday. Stop in on real estate company and especially for-sale-by-owner open houses. Pick up the flyer about the property from the outside signage or ask for one when you tour the property.

A vacant open house may be the quickest best deal for your buyer. Ask questions of the real estate agent or seller holding the open house. Inform them you are working as a buyer's agent. Tell them the buyers are prepared to make them an offer quickly if the property fits their parameters.

New Builder Homes
In some areas, it seems buyers are flocking to new construction like never before. Now that you have a committed buyer, you no longer lose them to the builder's reps. When the rep or builder says they don't pay fees or commissions, you can tell them that's fine because the buyer pays your fee.

And if your buyer gets lucky, some builders will say they will pay you a fee or bonus. You can be a fiduciary for the buyer helping them in the transaction. Not only is this better for your buyer, but it actually helps take some of the load off the builder's rep as well because there are usually not enough of them in busy areas.

So where are we now? You have used the best methods for you to find the best possible deals that fit your buyer's parameters. You have shown the best properties to your buyer. Your buyer has made their favorite choice. It is now time to get the best possible price and terms for your excited buyer. Like in the new home deal, this may mean you are working with a builder's rep or, most likely, a seller's agent.

In the next chapter, we are going to talk about making money working with buyers. We will look at getting paid on an hourly basis to assist a buyer in various parts of the real estate transaction. We will also talk about making money working with buyers, before, during, and after the closing.

CHAPTER 15

Making Money Working with Buyers

This chapter is designed to take you farther into the process of making money working with buyers. It expands the new buyers paradigm. It also delivers on our promise of how to double your real estate commissions working with buyers. This chapter will be especially important to your cash flow as we move farther into a normal real estate market.

We are going to present ideas and examples that we hope will have you think about new ways to make money working with buyers. Our goal is to stimulate you to go beyond what we are presenting here and come up with your own ideas about making money in your real estate business.

In the new buyers paradigm, you can make money working with a buyer locating a property for them. You can make money working with a buyer after the buyer has already found a property that the buyer wants to buy and they want you to present an offer for them.

You can also make money working with a buyer after the buyer has found a property and made an offer that has been accepted by the seller. The buyer may just want you to handle all the details of the closing.

Three Main Areas Working with Buyers

There are three main areas that we have identified in which you can make money working with buyers. These three main

181

areas are locating the property, negotiating the transaction, and closing the escrow. There are other opportunities to make money working with buyers besides these three main areas. We will explore them later in this chapter. Let's look at the three main areas first, starting with locating the property.

Locating the Property

Some of you will become professional property locators. You will make money strictly in the locating-property area of the real estate business. You will meet with a client and make a locating-the-property presentation. You will ask the client for, and receive, a retainer that will be applied to your hourly rate for locating property.

Internet Guru

Locating the property may have a special appeal to those of you who we call Internet gurus. You are so proficient at finding information or tracking down details on the Internet. You may be able to turn this skill into a niche real estate consulting business.

Locating-the-Property Presentation

The locating-the-property presentation is a variation of the buyer listing presentation. You have to set and prepare for an appointment. You will need a minimum of an hour and a half. We recommend you plan for two hours.

The best place to meet with the client is at the client's home. As we previously have said, we like meeting with the client at the client's home so we can see what kind of property the client lives in. We also want to see the condition of the property. This way we can know what expectations the client is bringing to the search for their next property.

Preparing for the Appointment

Once you have made an appointment with the client, you need to prepare for the appointment. The client may have informed you that they just want your services in the locating-the-property arena. However, you need to be prepared to make a complete buyer listing presentation.

Why, you ask? Because there may be tens of thousands of dollars of real estate commissions on the client's kitchen table. After all, why would the client want your help in locating a property unless the client was serious about making a real estate purchase?

What to Bring to the Appointment

Bring the five items to the locating-the-property appointment that you would bring to the buyer listing presentation. The number one thing to bring to the locating-the-property appointment is you *being* a real estate professional. You also bring your personalized buyer listing presentation notebook, buyer listing agreements, your laptop computer, and your calendar.

At the Appointment

You want to conduct the appointment as if you are making a complete buyer listing presentation. After arriving, ask the client to give you a tour of their home. Then you would say the following:

Mr. Client, thank you so much for showing me your home. I would like to take a few minutes and show you how I propose we work together to find your next home. Would that be all right with you?

After Mr. Client says yes, begin your buyer listing presentation. This can be in your presentation notebook or on your laptop. Go over with the client that it is your company policy to exclusively represent buyers in a real estate transaction when a written buyer listing agreement is in place. You should then state as a fact that the real estate buyer pays real estate commissions because the real estate buyer is the party in the transaction with the money.

Letters of Recommendation

It is imperative for your success that you include letters of recommendation from former clients that you can show to the prospective client. This will have the client feel comfortable that you can do a great job for him. Next, we recommend you spend some time on agency disclosure.

Agency Disclosure

We feel giving agency disclosure is the most important step in the buyer listing presentation or in any of the client consulting presentations. We are including here some of the actual buyer listing presentation materials we gave you in Chapter 6 to refresh your memory. You may use one, two, or all three of the following paragraphs in your locating-the-property presentation.

1. Mr. Client, it is my company policy to work for you exclusively in your upcoming real estate purchase. That way, I can find you the perfect property for the price you want to pay and with the terms that you can best afford. Would that be all right with you?

2. Mr. Client, I want to give you some information about real estate brokerage services. This will take just a few minutes. After you see this information, I think you will agree that what will be in your best interest is for me to represent you exclusively in the purchase of your next home. Would you like to see this information?

3. Mr. Client, in a real estate transaction, the seller can be represented, the buyer can be represented, or the seller and buyer can be represented. While there are several different combinations of representation that may occur, I prefer to keep it simple. I will exclusively represent you as the buyer in the purchase of your next home. Would that be all right with you?

Whether you use paragraphs one, two, or all three, what is important is to elicit yes responses from Mr. Client. You are setting the stage for what is next in your presentation.

Types of Property You Can Find for the Client

This is the part of your locating-the-property presentation in which you will have Mr. Client wanting to retain your services. Everything is available to you and Mr. Client when you have a consulting contract in place.

This would include the property that is seller-listed with your company, property seller-listed by other brokers, and all the rest of the open market. As we said in Chapter 14, there are more properties on the open market than there are listed with brokers.

We suggest you give Mr. Client the proverbial drink out of the fire hydrant.

Mr. Client, properties are everywhere! Once we have our agreement in place, I can do whatever needs to be done to find the best property and the best deal for you. Unlike normal real estate agents who have access only to their company listings or other real estate company listings, I have access to everything.

I do my own scouting of open houses, abandoned properties, and new builder developments. I track for sale by owners by their signage and their newspaper ads and Internet ads. I also find properties from ads that I place.

I track foreclosures by searching the public record and through a foreclosure service I subscribe to. This includes VA, FHA, Fannie Mae, and Freddie Mac foreclosures.

In fact Mr. Client, you can bring to my attention any property that you are interested in purchasing. I can help with property that is on the market or off the market. I will be able to find you the perfect property once I know and keep updated in writing what kind of property you want. Would that be all right with you?

Ask for the Order

Now is the perfect time to ask for the order. We recommend going for the full buyer listing. Take out your buyer listing agreement and begin to fill it out. When you get to the section on type of property to be acquired say the following:

Mr. Client, I would like to write down exactly the parameters of the property you are looking for. Would that be all right with you?

After you have the client's property parameters written down, say the following:

Mr. Client, I know that I will be able to find the perfect property for you. I also will be able to write an offer for you, present your offer, and negotiate for the best price and terms for you. May I ask who is going to

write your offer, present your offer, and negotiate on your
behalf after I find the perfect property?

Listen carefully to what Mr. Client says. This is where
you will find out if there is a real estate licensee that Mr. Client has available in his hip pocket. Whether Mr. Client has a
real estate license or has a friend or relative with a real estate
license, you are still going to ask for an exclusive buyer listing
agreement.

**Mr. Client, I can appreciate you wanting to use your
Uncle George to write the offer for you. Why are you having me and not Uncle George locate the perfect property
for you?**

It does not matter what Mr. Client says. He could say
Uncle George is part-time and would not be able to spend a
lot of time looking for property. He could say Uncle George
is retired but still has his real estate license. He could say he
wants to do Uncle George a favor.

**Mr. Client, the bottom line is you have some reserva-
tions about Uncle George being able to find the perfect
property for you. Do I understand you correctly?**

After Mr. Client agrees with your assessment that he has
some reservations about Uncle George finding him the perfect property, say the following:

**Mr. Client, if you have reservations about Uncle
George finding you property, do you have any reservations about Uncle George getting you a great deal at the
negotiating table?**

When Mr. Client admits to having reservations about
Uncle George getting him a great deal at the negotiating
table, you have your opening to ask for the exclusive buyer
listing.

**Mr. Client, I recommend we put together a buyer
listing agreement. Then I will be able to find you the perfect property, negotiate a great deal for you, and handle
the transaction all the way through to a successful closing.
Would that be all right with you?**

Congratulations, Mr. Client will either agree to a buyer
listing agreement or a consulting agreement for you to locate
the property for him. Let's look at the next area to make
money working with a buyer.

Negotiating the Transaction

Some of you will become professional real estate transaction negotiators. You will make money strictly in the negotiating-the-transaction area of the real estate business. You will meet with a buyer and make a negotiating-the-transaction presentation. You will ask the buyer for and receive a retainer that will be applied to your hourly rate for being a negotiator.

Preparing for the Appointment

You will prepare for the negotiating-the-transaction appointment in the same way you prepare for a buyer listing appointment and a locating-the-property appointment. The buyer may have informed you that they just want your services in the negotiating-the-transaction arena. However, you need to be prepared to make a complete buyer listing presentation.

You will bring the five items to the negotiating-the-transaction appointment that you would bring to the buyer listing presentation. This would include you *being* a real estate professional, your personalized buyer listing presentation notebook, buyer listing agreements, your laptop computer, and your calendar.

Negotiating-the-Transaction Presentation

The negotiating-the-transaction presentation is a variation of the buyer listing presentation. A client comes to you after finding a property. The client pays you to write, present, and negotiate an offer for them. Essentially, the buyer wants you to negotiate the transaction.

After you have negotiated the offer, the buyer and seller can do the closing with or without your assistance. If the buyer needs your assistance in closing the escrow, you will charge an additional fee. We will talk about closing the escrow in the next section.

At the Appointment

We will assume you are at the appointment with the buyer. The buyer has already found a property that they want to buy. Obviously, you do not need to make the locating-the-property portion of the buyer listing presentation.

However, you do need to take the negotiating-the-transaction presentation from the beginning. After you have exchanged pleasantries with the buyer at the kitchen table, begin your presentation.

Mr. Client, thank you for inviting me into your home. My understanding is you have found your next home and would like my expertise in writing, presenting, and negotiating your offer for that home. I would like to take a few minutes and show you how I propose we work together to get the best deal possible for you on your next home. Would that be all right with you?

After Mr. Client says yes, begin your negotiating-the-transaction presentation. This can be in your presentation notebook or on your laptop. Go over with the client that it is your company policy to exclusively represent buyers in a real estate transaction when a written buyer listing agreement is in place. You should then state as a fact that the real estate buyer pays real estate commissions because the real estate buyer is the party in the transaction with the money.

Letters of Recommendation

It is imperative for your success that you include letters of recommendation from former clients that you can show to the prospective client. This will have the client feel comfortable that you can do a great job for him. Next, we recommend you spend some time on agency disclosure.

Agency Disclosure

We feel giving agency disclosure is the most important step in the buyer listing presentation or in any of the client consulting presentations.

Mr. Client, it is my company policy to work for you exclusively in your upcoming real estate purchase. That way, I can negotiate the best possible price and terms for you in this transaction. Would that be all right with you?

Now comes the part of your negotiating-the-transaction presentation in which you will have Mr. Client wanting to retain your services. Every negotiating tool in the book is available to you and Mr. Client when you have a consulting contract in place.

This includes all cash offers, conventional financing offers, Veterans Administration (VA) and Federal Housing Administration (FHA) offers, and seller financing offers. You can help them with offers on foreclosures, bank repossessions, and short-sale foreclosure offers. And you can write, present, and negotiate offers on every type of property out there. Again, we suggest you give Mr. Client the proverbial drink out of the fire hydrant.

Mr. Client, we will first determine your financial parameters. Based on these parameters, I will write an offer that gives you the best deal possible on your next home and makes the most sense financially for you. Once we have our agreement in place, I can do whatever needs to be done to negotiate the best deal for you.

Mr. Client, I have a complete understanding of real estate values in the area in which you have located your next home. I can guarantee you will know the market value of this property or any other property you are interested in before we write an offer.

Mr. Client, I am an expert negotiator. I can negotiate directly with the seller as in this for-sale-by-owner property you have found. I can also negotiate with attorneys, real estate agents, and banks on your behalf for whatever type of property you would like to buy.

Mr. Client, I can even negotiate with real estate lenders to get you the best interest rates and monthly payments if you decide to obtain new financing. Would that be all right with you?

Ask for the Order

Now is the perfect time to ask for the order. We recommend going for the full buyer listing. Take out your buyer listing agreement and begin to fill it out. You may not be able to negotiate an acceptable offer for Mr. Client on the property he has already located.

By having the buyer listing agreement in place, you can then begin your search for another property without having to go back to Mr. Client and put together another agreement.

So when you get to the section on type of property to be acquired say the following:

Mr. Client, while I know you have already found a property you would like to buy, I would like to write down exactly the parameters of the property you are looking for. Would that be all right with you?

After you have the client's property parameters written down, say the following:

Mr. Client, let's talk about the financial parameters next. Please tell me the price range, down payment, and monthly payment you would be comfortable with on the property you have found. Would that be all right with you?

After you have the client's financial parameters written down, say the following:

Mr. Client, I recommend we put together a buyer listing agreement. I know that I will be able to write an offer for you, present your offer, and negotiate for the best price and terms for you on the property you have found.

If for whatever reason you are not happy with the deal, we can go to another property. By having a buyer listing agreement in place, we will not miss a beat. Then I will be able to find you the perfect property, negotiate a great deal for you, and handle the transaction all the way through to a successful closing. Would that be all right with you?

Congratulations, Mr. Client will either agree to a buyer listing agreement or a consulting agreement for you to negotiate the transaction for him. Let's look at the next area to make money working with a buyer.

Closing the Escrow

Some of you will become professional closing-the-escrow experts. You will make money strictly by handling all the details involved in the closing-the-escrow area of the real estate business.

You will meet with a buyer and make a closing-the-escrow presentation. You will ask the buyer for and receive a retainer that will be applied to your hourly rate for being a closing-the-escrow expert.

Closing-the-Escrow Presentation

The closing-the-escrow presentation is a variation of the buyer listing presentation. A client comes to you after finding a property and negotiating an accepted offer. The client pays you to handle all the details involved in closing an escrow.

This is different than what the escrow officer or closing entity does. We are talking here about all the conditions that have to be met in order for the escrow to close.

Preparing for the Appointment

You will prepare for the closing-the-escrow appointment in the same way you prepare for a buyer listing appointment. The buyer may have informed you that they just want your services in the closing-the-escrow arena. However, you need to be prepared to make a complete buyer listing presentation.

You will bring the same five items to the closing-the-escrow appointment that you would bring to the buyer listing presentation. This would include you *being* a real estate professional, your personalized buyer listing presentation notebook, buyer listing agreements, your laptop computer, and your calendar.

At the Appointment

We will assume you are at the appointment with the buyer. The buyer has already found a property that they want to buy and have had an offer accepted by the seller. Obviously, you do not need to make the locating-the-property or the negotiating-the-transaction portion of the buyer listing presentation.

However, you do need to take the closing-the-escrow presentation from the beginning. After you have exchanged pleasantries with the buyer at the kitchen table, begin your presentation.

Mr. Client, thank you for inviting me into your home. My understanding is you have found your next home and have had an offer accepted by the seller. You would like my expertise in closing the escrow.

I would like to take a few minutes and show you how I propose we work together so I can help close the escrow on your next home. Would that be all right with you?

After Mr. Client says yes, begin your negotiating-the-transaction presentation. You will use the same steps as all the other presentations. The presentation can be from your notebook or on your laptop. You go over with the client that it is your company policy to exclusively represent buyers in a real estate transaction when a written buyer listing agreement is in place.

You should then state as a fact that the real estate buyer pays real estate commissions because the real estate buyer is the party in the transaction with the money. You then display your letters of recommendation and do agency disclosure.

Mr. Client, it is my company policy to work for you exclusively in your real estate purchase. That way, I can make sure the closing goes smoothly for you. Would that be all right with you?

Now comes the part of your closing-the-escrow presentation in which you will have Mr. Client wanting to retain your services. You will be able to handle all the details that have to be coordinated for the client for their side of the escrow.

You can handle the lender, the property inspector, the title reports, the escrow instructions. You can monitor the seller side of the escrow to make sure the seller is carrying out their responsibilities. You stay on top of the escrow officer and the client.

Mr. Client, I will handle everything that needs to be coordinated to successfully close your escrow. The escrow company and the escrow officer will handle the actual escrow closing.

I will make sure the lender, the title insurance company, the escrow officer, the property inspectors, the appraiser, and even the seller are doing their part. I will go over the escrow instructions with you so you are completely clear about what you are signing. Would that be all right with you? (Note: When it comes time for covering the final documents with them, you must remind them that you are not an attorney and if they think they need one, they should hire one to take a final look at the documents.)

Ask for the Order

Now is the perfect time to ask for the order. We recommend going for the full buyer listing. Take out your buyer listing agreement and begin to fill it out. The escrow on the current deal may fall out.

By having the buyer listing agreement in place, you can then begin your search for another property without having to go back to Mr. Client and put together another agreement.

Mr. Client, I recommend we put together a buyer listing agreement. I know that I will be able to coordinate a successful closing for you. But if, for whatever reason, you are not happy about anything that is revealed during the closing, we can go to another property.

By having a buyer listing agreement in place, we will not miss a beat. Then I will be able to find you the perfect property, negotiate a great deal for you, and handle the transaction all the way through to a successful closing. Would that be all right with you?

Congratulations, Mr. Client will either agree to a buyer listing agreement or a consulting agreement for you to close the escrow for him. Let's look at other opportunities to make money working with a buyer.

Other Opportunities to Make Money

There are several other ways to make money as a buyer's agent/consultant. Beyond the three main areas we have already discussed, there are several more. New, creative areas are popping up in the real estate industry all the time. But let's start with consulting.

Consulting

Some of you will create a consulting niche as the main focus of your real estate business. There are many areas you could choose to consult in. We think one of the biggest consulting niches will be in the area of researching value.

Researching Value

Some of you may decide to become appraisers. That is fine with us. But that is not what we are talking about here. After all, where does an appraiser get the data for making their appraisal?

Besides getting closed property information at title companies that nonappraisers don't have access to or appraisal records from various sources, appraisers get their data from real estate agents who are operating in the marketplace.

You know the kind of data we are talking about. Data from real estate agents like market comparisons sold, pending sales, current listings, expired listings, and number of days on the market. Home buyers or other clients such as real estate investors may not want to hire an appraiser because appraisers make an aftermarket analysis. Real estate agents make an in-the-market real estate market evaluation.

Other Consulting

We will conclude our making money with buyers discussion by mentioning three more areas. We actually described this chapter way back in the Table of Contents "You can make money working with buyers before, during, or after the closing."

You can make money before the closing being a hard-money lender financing a buyer's real estate investment. You can make money during the closing as an investor partner with a buyer. And you can make money after the closing by being an expert witness for a buyer in a legal dispute.

In the next chapter, we will have a conversation about implementing a professional program to list buyers. Our focus will be directed toward real estate company owners, brokers of record, and office managers. If you are an associate licensee, you may be especially interested to see what may be going on in the near future in your company.

CHAPTER 16

Implementing a Professional Program to List Buyers

This chapter is about implementing a professional program to list buyers. This can be done by you, your office, or your company. Implementing this kind of program may require a decision by the company owner, company broker, or company office manager. If you asked us how to implement your professional program to list buyers, we have several answers to give you.

Our first answer is to contact us! We are available on a consulting or training basis to get you up and running. Our second answer is to get some consulting or training through your company or some other well-regarded company in the field of buyer brokerage.

Our third answer is to read this chapter and incorporate our suggestions and recommendations. Whatever method you choose, what is important is that you implement the professional program to list buyers in the near future. Let's get started.

Some Things to Think About

We want to start out by giving you some things to think about. The more thinking and planning you do, the better chance of a smooth and successful implementation of your professional program to list buyers. Remember, change always causes upset. Anytime you introduce something new, some people are going to be upset.

Your job as the owner of your company, broker of record, or office manager is to make the tough decisions. You have to be constantly ahead of the curve both to keep your competitive edge and to protect yourself, your business, and your agents.

Courage on Your Part

The first thing we would like you to think about is courage. It may take some courage on your part to implement a new business practice with regard to buyers. Why do we say it may take some courage on your part to implement a professional program to list buyers? There are several reasons, but most especially our first.

You may encounter resistance from some of the old-timers and the agents who are comfortable with the old buyers paradigm. These could be some of your top producers and seller listing stars. They have been making lots of money working in the current paradigm, thank you very much. Their message to you will be "Do not rock the boat!"

The Approach

The approach we recommend you take is to emphasize the benefits of a new business practice with buyers to all the agents in your office. For the agents who are your seller listing stars, not much will change for them. They probably do not even want to work with buyers. Working with sellers has been their forte and will continue to be so even in a normal real estate market.

For the agents who work primarily with buyers and the newer agents in your office, implementing a professional program to list buyers will be fairly straightforward. You will show them how it works. You will show them how it makes them money. You will turn them loose.

Timing

The next thing you need to think about is the timing of implementing your new buyer listing program. *Time is of the essence* is on every real estate contract and agreement we have ever encountered. We recommend you announce the timing of the new program at least ninety days before you officially implement the program.

This will give everyone time to prepare for what is coming. Also it gives people time to be upset with the change and time to get over being upset with the change!

And finally, it gives people time to ask questions, give the idea a road test so to speak, and make some suggestions and improvements. This gives your people a sense of having a say-so in what is coming. It gives them a chance to take ownership of the new policy.

Company Agency Policy

Speaking of policy, you may have to think or rethink what your company agency policy is going to be to accommodate your new listing buyers business model. Whatever your company agency policy is, the policy must be in writing.

This protects you, the other agents, and your buyer and seller clients. By having this policy in writing, you create the basis for training your agents in giving your state-mandated disclosure regarding real estate agency disclosure.

Let's review what your current company agency policy might be. For some of you, your current company agency policy may already accommodate implementing your new business model. For others of you, your company agency policy may need to be modified or in some cases completely changed.

There is no right answer here. You have to think about what is going to be the best company policy for your real estate business as we move forward over the next five to ten years in a normal market. Just keep in mind, it will be better for you to be proactive rather than reactive in this arena.

The following is a partial detailing of some possible company agency policies. We will comment on how listing buyers will or will not fit into or with each of the agency policies we present. Listing buyers will work better with some agency policies than with others. You may have to invent your own company agency policy.

Seller Single Agency

Your company agency policy is seller single agency. You have a company focus to make money listing sellers. It is not that you will not work with buyers. You just prefer working with sellers.

How Seller Single Agency Works

Let's see how seller single agency works. We will start with your company as the seller listing agent. We will then see what happens when an associate licensee from your company presents an offer on your company's seller listing. Next, we will look at when an outside company's associate licensee presents an offer on your company's seller listing.

Then we will look at your company as the selling agent on an outside company's seller listing. Finally, we will give you our analysis of seller single agency as a company agency policy with regard to implementing a professional program to list buyers.

Your Company as Seller Listing Agent

An associate licensee in your company takes a seller listing. Your company policy is to represent the seller exclusively in the real estate transaction. The seller is represented by an agent acting as a fiduciary (the broker of record for your company) through the associate licensee who took the listing.

Your Company Presents an Offer

If the associate licensee who took the listing or another associate licensee in your company presents an offer on your company's seller listing, your company represents the seller exclusively. The buyer is not represented by an agent acting as a fiduciary in this situation. There is no buyer representation.

Outside Company Presents an Offer

If an outside company's associate licensee presents an offer on your company's seller listing, your company represents the seller exclusively. The outside company can also represent the seller exclusively as your company's subagent. The buyer is not represented by an agent acting as a fiduciary in this situation. There is no buyer representation.

Your Company as Selling Agent

An associate licensee in your company presents an offer on an outside company's seller listing. Your company policy is to represent the seller exclusively in the real estate transaction. The seller is represented by an agent acting as a fiduciary (the broker of record for the outside company) through the associate licensee of the outside company who took the listing.

The seller is also represented by a subagent acting as a fiduciary (the broker of record for your company) through the associate licensee of your company who presents the offer. The buyer is not represented by an agent acting as a fiduciary in this situation. There is no buyer representation. Again, you can have the buyer sign a buyer nonagency agreement.

Our Analysis

Seller single agency means exactly what it says. If this is your company agency policy, your emphasis, by definition, is representing sellers. You would have to make a complete business model shift to represent buyers the way we have talked about in this book. Seller single agency as a company policy precludes ever being a fiduciary of the buyer.

List Buyers

You can still list buyers, however. You can have the buyer sign a buyer nonagency agreement. In that agreement, you inform the buyer that you are exclusively representing the seller in any real estate transaction.

The buyer is welcome to make an offer on any of your seller listings or any other company's seller listings. An associate licensee in your company could even present an offer on a new builder home or a for sale by owner.

It is even possible to have the buyer agree to pay you a real estate commission or an hourly consulting fee. Remember, who pays a real estate commission and who receives a real estate commission does not determine agency!

Dual Agency for In-House Sales/Single Agency Otherwise

Your company agency policy is to be a dual agent when you sell one of your own seller listings. You will represent the seller exclusively when an outside company sells one of your seller listings. You will represent the buyer exclusively when you sell an outside company's seller listing.

How Dual Agency In-House/Single Agency Otherwise Works

Let's see how dual agency in-house/single agency otherwise works. We will start with your company as the seller listing agent. We will then see what happens when an associate licensee from your company presents an offer on your company's seller listing. Next, we will look at when an outside company's associate licensee presents an offer on your company's seller listing.

Then we will look at your company as the selling agent on an outside company's seller listing. Finally, we will give you our analysis of dual agency in-house/single agency otherwise as a company agency policy with regard to implementing a professional program to list buyers.

Your Company as Seller Listing Agent

An associate licensee in your company takes a seller listing. Your company policy is to represent the seller and the buyer (dual agency) if you sell the listing in-house. The seller is represented by an agent acting as a fiduciary (the broker of record for your company) through the associate licensee who took the listing. The buyer is represented by an agent acting as a fiduciary (the broker of record for your company) through the associate licensee who presents the offer.

Your Company Presents an Offer

If the associate licensee who took the listing or another associate licensee in your company presents an offer on your company's seller listing, your company represents the seller and the buyer as dual agents.

Outside Company Presents an Offer

If an outside company's associate licensee presents an offer on your company's seller listing, your company represents the seller exclusively. The outside company represents the buyer exclusively. The seller is represented by an agent acting as a fiduciary (the broker of record for your company) through the associate licensee who took the listing. The buyer is represented by an agent acting as a fiduciary (the broker of record for the outside company) through the outside associate licensee who presents the offer.

Your Company as Selling Agent

An associate licensee in your company presents an offer on an outside company's seller listing. Your company policy is to represent the buyer exclusively in the real estate transaction. The seller is represented by an agent acting as a fiduciary (the broker of record for the outside company) through the associate licensee of the outside company who took the listing. The buyer is represented by an agent acting as a fiduciary (the broker of record for your company) through the associate licensee who presents the offer.

Our Analysis

Your company agency policy is to represent buyers exclusively when you are selling another company's seller listings. You need to implement a professional program to list buyers for this portion of your business.

Dual Agency All the Time

Your company agency policy is to be a dual agent all the time. You are a dual agent when you sell one of you own seller listings. You are a dual agent when you sell an outside company's seller listings.

How Dual Agency All the Time Works

Let's see how dual agency all the time works. We will start with your company as the seller listing agent. We will then see what happens when an associate licensee from your company presents an offer on your company's seller listing. Next, we will look at when an outside company's associate licensee presents an offer on your company's seller listing.

Then we will look at your company as the selling agent on an outside company's seller listing. Finally, we will give you our analysis of dual agency all the time as a company agency policy with regard to implementing a professional program to list buyers.

Your Company as Seller Listing Agent

An associate licensee in your company takes a seller listing. Your company policy is to represent the seller and the buyer (dual agency) if you sell the listing in-house. The seller is represented by an agent acting as a fiduciary (the broker of record for your company) through the associate licensee who took the listing. The buyer is represented by an agent acting as a fiduciary (the broker of record for your company) through the associate licensee who presents the offer.

Your Company Presents an Offer

If the associate licensee who took the listing or another associate licensee in your company presents an offer on your company's seller listing, your company represents the seller and the buyer as dual agents.

Outside Company Presents an Offer

Your company policy also is to represent the seller and the buyer (dual agency) if an outside company presents an offer. The seller is represented by an agent acting as a fiduciary (the broker of record for your company) through the associate licensee who took the listing, The seller also is represented by an agent acting as a fiduciary (the broker of record for the outside company) through the outside associate licensee who presents the offer.

The buyer is represented by an agent acting as a fiduciary (the broker of record for your company) through the associate licensee who took the listing. The buyer is also represented by an agent acting as a fiduciary (the broker of record for the outside company) through the outside associate licensee who presents the offer.

Your Company as Selling Agent

An associate licensee in your company presents an offer on an outside company's seller listing. Your company policy is to represent the buyer and the seller (dual agency) in the real estate transaction. The seller is represented by an agent acting as a fiduciary (the broker of record for the outside company) through the associate licensee of the outside company who took the listing.

The buyer is represented by an agent acting as a fiduciary (the broker of record for your company) through the associate licensee of your company who presents the offer.

Our Analysis

Your company agency policy is to be a dual agent all the time. We think this is an untenable company agency policy. As we have said, we think dual agency's days are numbered. Our recommendation is to move away from any form of dual agency as a company policy, agency or otherwise.

However, you can implement a buyer listing program. This might actually afford you some protection for your dual agency policy. You can show that you list buyers as well as sellers. You treat buyers in the same manner that you treat sellers.

Buyer Single Agency

Your company agency policy is buyer single agency. You have a company focus to make money listing buyers. It is not that you will not work with sellers. You just prefer working with buyers.

How Buyer Single Agency Works

Let's see how buyer single agency works. We will start with your company as the buyer listing agent. We will then see what happens when an associate licensee from your company presents an offer on your company's seller listing. Next, we will look at when an outside company's associate licensee presents an offer on your company's seller listing.

Then we will look at your company as the selling agent on an outside company's seller listing. Finally, we will give you our

analysis of buyer single agency as a company agency policy with
regard to implementing a professional program to list buyers.

Your Company as Seller Listing Agent

An associate licensee in your company takes a seller listing.
Your company policy is to represent the buyer exclusively in
the real estate transaction. The seller is *not* represented by an
agent acting as a fiduciary (the broker of record for your company) through the associate licensee who took the listing.

Your Company Presents an Offer

If the associate licensee who took the listing or another associate licensee in your company presents an offer on your
company's seller listing, your company represents the buyer
exclusively. The seller is not represented by an agent acting as
a fiduciary in this situation. There is no seller representation.

Outside Company Presents an Offer

If an outside company's associate licensee presents an offer on
your company's seller listing, your company represents no one
in the transaction. The outside company represents the buyer
exclusively. The seller is not represented by an agent acting as
a fiduciary in this situation. There is no seller representation.

Alternate Policies

Your company could allow the outside company to be a dual
agent representing the seller and the buyer in the transaction.

Or your company could allow the outside company to
represent the seller exclusively.

And/or your company could represent the buyer exclusively.

Your Company as Selling Agent

An associate licensee in your company presents an offer on
an outside company's seller listing. Your company policy is to
represent the buyer exclusively in the real estate transaction.
The seller is represented by an agent acting as a fiduciary (the
broker of record for the outside company) through the associate licensee of the outside company who took the listing.

The buyer is represented by an agent acting as a fiduciary (the broker of record for your company) through the associate licensee of your company who presents the offer.

Our Analysis

Buyer single agency means exactly what it says. If this is your company agency policy, your emphasis, by definition, is representing buyers. Buyer single agency as a company policy precludes ever being a fiduciary of the seller. You have already implemented or are about to implement your professional program to list buyers.

List Sellers

You can still list sellers, however. You can have the seller sign a seller nonagency agreement. In that agreement, you inform the seller that you are exclusively representing the buyer in any real estate transaction. It is even possible to have the seller agree to pay you a real estate commission because who pays a real estate commission and who receives a real estate commission does not determine agency!

Now the agency conversation is clear. You have decided where the company policy stands. You have a written company policy that may or may not need some updating. You are ready to move the company forward. It is now time to implement your professional program to list buyers.

Implement Your Professional Program to List Buyers

So how do you get started on implementing your new program? Here are our recommended five steps to follow to implement your professional program to list buyers. The first step is thinking about your buyer listing program. The second step is the timing of introducing the program. The third step is training your agents to be successful with the program. The fourth step is tooling up to launch the program. The fifth step is tweaking the program in its early stages as you discover what is working and what is not working.

Step 1: Thinking

We have suggested several things to think about regarding your buyer listing program. We mentioned you thinking about having the courage to introduce a buyer listing program. How are you going to handle the agents who are going to be upset at the changes this new business model will introduce?

Are you going to require all your agents to work the buyer listing program? Or are you going to let your seller listing superstars stay exclusively with the seller listings?

You are going to have to think about what kind of a company agency policy you will choose to make your buyer listing program the most effective. And who are you going to have conduct your training once you decide to implement the program? Are you going to handle the training in-house or are you going to go outside the company?

Step 2: Timing

We mentioned timing as something to think about. We suggested you have at least a 90-day period between announcing the program and implementing the program. This gives people time to get used to the idea.

What is the best time to introduce the program? We recommend you introduce the program as quickly as possible. Some companies prefer to introduce business model changes in the traditional off-peak times of fall and winter. We disagree.

We think introducing your buyer listing program whenever it is practical is the best time. If this means you introduce the program in spring or summer, so be it. That way, you can get a real feel for how the program is going to work.

Step 3: Training

Training is critical for your buyer listing program to be successful. As we have said, the approach we recommend you take is to emphasize the benefits of a new business practice with buyers to all the agents in your office.

The training for the new program must include making clear your company's agency policy, giving your state's current mandated agency disclosure, and making a buyer listing presentation. The training also should include how to communicate your new buyer listing program to the other real estate companies in your area that you do business with.

For the agents who work primarily with buyers and the newer agents in your office, training them to list buyers will be fairly straightforward. You will show them how it works. You will show them how it makes them money. They will begin listing buyers.

Step 4: Tooling Up

Tooling up actually will run parallel with training. What buyer listing agreements are you going to use? Are you going to ask for retainers? Are the retainers you ask for going to be nonrefundable? Do you need a separate broker's trust account for buyer retainers?

Will you have to change the real estate contracts you use to write offers? What kind of advertising will you do? Can you get some free PR from the local media about your new buyer program? What changes will you have to make to your company web site?

Step 5: Tweaking

Tweaking may be the most important step of the five steps in implementing the program. Until you road test your buyer listing program in the marketplace, you really do not know how it is going to work.

Being flexible is the name of the game in introducing any new business model. No matter how much time and money you have put into launching this program, you have to be ready to take the feedback. This may mean tweaking or even discarding parts of the program that you really want to keep.

For example, you may find resistance in your marketplace to nonrefundable retainers. You find that buyers are willing to sign buyer listing agreements with your agents and even write a check for a retainer. The buyers are balking at the nonrefundable aspect, however.

Be flexible. For those buyers who are uncomfortable with the nonrefundable aspect of the retainer, have your agents offer to have it be refundable minus the hourly minimum accrued and expenses incurred for the first 30 days of the buyer listing period.

Also, you may need to tweak your program based on feedback from your agents. You may start out the program not giving them any portion of the nonrefundable retainer. They have to wait till escrow closes in order to get paid.

You may decide that in order to inject some excitement into the program, you will sweeten the pot. You tweak the program by offering your agents their commission split of the nonrefundable retainer the Friday after the buyer's retainer check clears.

We know you have lots of questions about implementing a buyer listing program. Some of you have already implemented very successful buyer listing programs. If you have found something that works, then good for you. Just have the courage to keep tweaking your program for continued success.

We are going to close this book with a chapter on the future of the real estate industry. We are really hoping that we are opening a new chapter for you and your real estate business.

CHAPTER 17

The Future of the Real Estate Industry

Welcome to a completely professional real estate industry. That sounds really good to us. How does it sound to you? In this chapter, we will give you our thoughts on the future of the real estate industry. We will do this from a perspective of making predictions based on where the real estate industry is today and where we believe it will go in the future.

We are going to paint the picture of a possible future real estate industry. There may be nothing in existence today that would make what we present here seem predictable as a possible future for the real estate industry.

It will be up to you if you think this is a future real estate industry that you would like to have in existence. If it is something you want to have as part of your real estate industry legacy, then we invite you to help build this future.

We are going to talk about this subject from three perspectives. The first perspective will be the real estate industry of the future. The second perspective will be the real estate home owner of the future. The third perspective will be the real estate buyer of the future.

The Real Estate Industry of the Future

The real estate industry of the future will be built on strategic alliances and the bundling of services. There is so much money involved in the real estate industry that some very large players have become involved in the game. These players will define what strategic alliances are put in place in the future.

To give you a sense of the money involved in the real estate industry is practically impossible. The value of residential real estate in 2005 was $18.6 trillion. That is trillion with a letter *t*. This was $3 trillion more than the value held in domestic stocks!

2005 Value of Residential Real Estate

$18,600,000,000,000

By 2025, we estimate the value of residential real estate will be $100 trillion.

2025 Value of Residential Real Estate

$100,000,000,000,000

Strategic Alliances

We began this book talking about the real estate industry of one hundred years ago. We said that the people who were in the real estate business were in the insurance business first and foremost. Real estate was just an adjunct business to their insurance business.

In the real estate industry of the future, strategic alliances will be formed that will have the real estate business be the major focus. Let's take a look at one of the strategic alliances that is already happening in our area. We know these same types of strategic alliances are occurring in your area.

Bank of America and Century 21 Mike Bowman, Inc.

The following information was taken from a public relations piece in the real estate section of our local newspaper. Although it may look like we are doing a commercial for Bank of America and Century 21 Mike Bowman, Inc., one of the largest real estate companies in the country, we assure you we are not. We are using them as an example of the size of the players involved.

("CENTURY 21 Mike Bowman forms new alliance with Bank of America," *Star-Telegram*, April 8, 2006. Reprint Courtesy of the Fort Worth *Star-Telegram*.) Bank of America and CENTURY 21 Mike Bowman Inc. have joined forces to make buying and selling a home easier, while saving clients thousands of dollars. Bank of America sees two major [paradigm] shifts taking place in the home ownership industry.

The first one is due to technology and the use of the Internet, making it easier for people to interface with mortgage lenders and real estate agents. The second is the building of home ownership services.

Bank of America wants to work closely with real estate brokers, builders, and corporate relocation providers who share their vision. That is why they have created a mutually beneficial alliance with CENTURY 21 Mike Bowman.

Bank of America is one of the leading providers of residential real estate financing in the country. Bank of America has the largest online customer base of any financial services company in the world. They average more than 600,000 unique users in a month on their Loans and Homes section of their Web site www.bankofamerica.com.

CENTURY 21 Mike Bowman is a real estate company on the cutting-edge of technology. Bowman's in-house technology department has developed its own real estate brokerage software along with an outstanding Web site.

CENTURY 21 Mike Bowman has made it possible for all visitors to the Bank of America Corporate Web site to view available homes for sale in the North Texas area. Bank of America customers receive special real estate discounts when they use CENTURY 21 Mike Bowman and Bank of America.

Mike Bowman, President of CENTURY 21 Mike Bowman, said "I'm excited about this relationship and the opportunity to offer buyers and sellers special real estate discounts and services that can save them thousands of dollars."

Do you think Mike Bowman could be talking about full-service real estate brokerage being provided by his company at a reduced commission to Bank of America customers? Do you think Century 21 Mike Bowman customers could receive loans from Bank of America at reduced interest rates and loan processing fees?

Bundling of Services

In the real estate industry of the future, bundling of services will be one of the outcomes of strategic alliances. Let's take a look at an example of the bundling of services that is already happening in our area. Again, we know this same bundling of services is occurring in your area.

Downtown Residential Resource Center

The following information was taken from a newspaper article in the business section of our local newspaper. Again, although it may look like we are doing a commercial for the Downtown Residential Resource Center, we assure you we are not.

We are using this as an example of the bundling of services that is occurring in the real estate industry. We found the headline of the article intriguing.

("Agents to Open 1-Stop Shop," *Star-Telegram*, January 17, 2006. Reprint Courtesy of the Fort Worth *Star-Telegram*.)

Agents to Open 1-Stop Shop

Bryan McDonald and Shad Green are partners in Fairway Properties, which builds custom homes for investors. The two are also real estate agents for Keller Williams, one of the area's largest residential brokerages.

They are opening the Downtown Residential Resource Center on the top two penthouse floors of a remodeled office building in the downtown area. The 15th floor will have offices for Fairway Properties, Keller Williams, Reunion Title, and a property and casualty insurance company. The 16th floor will have offices for the mortgage division of Bank of America and VIP Mortgage.

The Downtown Residential Resource Center will offer potential buyers, sellers, and renters of downtown properties a single place to turn for information and help. Buyers will be able to locate, finance, insure, and close deals at the center.

The idea behind the 10,000 square-foot center is to make it easier for prospective buyers to find all the information and help they need in one location. The information now is segmented among too many real-estate agencies, which can be cumbersome for buyers. "We will be attracting and representing prospective buyers for downtown projects and offering the one-stop, all-under-one-roof concept for the downtown market area," Bryan McDonald said.

So we have the bundling of buyer agents, custom home builders, a residential brokerage company, a title insurance company, a property and casualty insurance company, and two real estate lenders. This is all in a downtown, penthouse environment. And there is Bank of America, again. They always seem to be in the mix.

Real Estate Agents

To complete our perspective of the real estate industry of the future, we have to talk about the real estate agent of the future. After all, we say in the real estate industry that we are in the people business. The most important people in the real estate industry of the future are going to be the real estate agents.

In order for the real estate industry to have a future, we must attract the youngest and brightest. These will be the people that are educated, multiple-licensed, technologically sophisticated, well networked, and professional. They are people who are looking for a career. The real estate industry has to create a career path that offers long-term employment stability, the opportunity for advancement, and the potential to make a sizable income.

This means that we have to figure out as an industry how to mitigate the historical downturns and expand the historical upturns associated with being a real estate agent selling residential real estate. We have to have a residential real estate industry that creates a new paradigm beyond the feast or famine paradigm of the current real estate market.

Best Time to Get into the Real Estate Business

Stan Ross, who is the board chairman of the University of Southern California's Lusk Center for Real Estate, says that starting a real estate career when sales are slow actually can be a good thing. "There is a lot of opportunity for careers in real estate in lots of sectors: income-producing properties like apartments, office developers, industrial, retail, mixed-use in urban development," he said.

"As far as agents, it could be a very unique opportunity for the best in the lot. Your biggest issue is sales. Housing developers are examining their marketing strategies. They are looking for people who are really creative and enthusiastic. Obviously there are challenges," Ross added.

Passion for the Industry

Ross expressed his passion for the real estate industry in a recently published book that he coauthored with writer James Carberry called *The Inside Track to Careers in Real Estate* published by the Urban Land Institute (Washington, D.C., 2006). He is enthusiastic about the real estate industry despite flattening prices and growing inventories of unsold homes.

Ross disagrees with the thinking that some people have that real estate is a fallback career. He says that real estate is a calling. We like Stan Ross's thinking that real estate is a calling. We think that the real estate agent of the future will have to be called to the real estate profession. The requirements to be a real estate agent will be daunting to the faint of heart.

Multiple Licenses

The real estate agent of the future will be licensed in real estate, life and disability insurance, casualty insurance, tax preparation, securities, and auctioneering. The real estate agent of the future will be able to pull credit reports, do appraisals, issue title insurance, do real estate loans, and close escrows.

The Real Estate Home Owner of the Future

The real estate home owner of the future will be able to protect the value of their home against the cyclical downturns in the real estate market. They will be able to lock in favorable values by using futures contracts. Although most home owners are not familiar with the futures market, the futures market has been in existence for almost one hundred fifty years.

The futures markets were designed in the late 1880s to give farmers and ranchers price certainty on sales of their crops and livestock. A farmer can lock in a price today that they are willing to sell their soybean crop for three, six, or twelve months from now.

Hedge the Value of Homes

The idea that home owners should be able to hedge the value of their homes against falling prices has been around for many years. This is now a reality. The Chicago Mercantile Exchange began offering housing futures contracts in April 2006.

"The driving force behind the development of housing futures has been the boom of recent years," said John Labuszewski, managing director of research at the Chicago Mercantile Exchange, in November 2005. The national median home price value stood at $195,000 at the end of 2005. This was up 65 percent from 2000 to 2005. Some areas of the country experienced 100 percent to 200 percent median price increases in that same five-year period.

Risk

What has not been available in the housing market up till now is a mechanism for protecting against the risk of buying at the top of the real estate market. If you are the last real estate buyer in just before the market levels off or drops in value, you can experience quite a financial setback. "We tell people about risk in the stock market all the time," said Anthony Sanders, professor of finance at The Ohio State University. "But then when it comes to housing, which accounts for 90 percent of most people's portfolio, we don't say anything about risks."

How It Will Work

Housing futures contracts will begin by being offered on 10 housing indexes representing the median home prices in 10 cities. These cities are Boston, Chicago, Denver, Las Vegas, Los Angeles, Miami, New York, San Diego, San Francisco, and Washington, D.C.

What if you do not own real estate in one of these 10 cities? You may still want to protect the value of your real estate holdings if you feel the overall real estate market is in jeopardy of losing value. You could buy futures contracts in the housing markets you feel will have the most impact on your real estate market.

Example

The value of one New York futures contract would be determined by multiplying the New York index by, let's say, $240. The New York index would be determined on a daily basis by the buying and selling that occurs in the New York housing futures market.

This would be similar to what happens with the major stock indexes each day, which go up or down depending on who is buying and who is selling. The $240 figure would be set by a market maker in the New York futures housing market. If the current New York index is 254.32, then the contract value is $61,037.

New York Contract Value

New York Index	254.32
Multiplier	× $240
Contract Value	$61,037

Protect against a Loss

Let's say the owner of a $600,000 condominium in Manhattan thinks real estate values are going to fall in his market. To protect themselves against a loss, the condominium owner could sell 10 housing futures contracts. This would equal the value of the condominium.

Sell Futures Contracts

Contract Value	$61,037
Number of Contracts	× 10
Total Value	$610,370

Performance Bond

A futures contracts investor has to make a performance bond deposit of 5 percent of the total value of the contract. The bond is a way to prepay for any loss that the investor might have on the contract if prices move in the wrong direction.

The wrong direction is relative. If you buy futures contracts because you think the market is going to drop and it goes up, the futures contracts may be worthless. But your asset is worth more!

In our example, the condominium owner would have to put up a performance bond of approximately $3,000, or 5 percent of the $61,037 for each contract. For 10 contracts, this would be approximately $30,000.

Performance Bond

Amount per Contract	$3,000
Number of Contracts	× 10
Performance Bond	$30,000

Past Declines

Although home and condominium values have risen dramatically over the last five years, several sharp value declines have occurred in the past. Boston home and condominium values fell 29 percent between 1987 and 1994. Los Angeles values fell 41 percent between 1989 and 1997. This is according to a report by the Chicago Mercantile Exchange.

Current Decline

Let's say the Manhattan real estate market crashes. The $600,000 condominium loses $180,000 in value. The condominium then would be worth only $420,000.

Condominium Loses Value

Owner Paid	$600,000
Value Loss	– $180,000
New Value	$420,000

Sell Futures Contracts

By selling three of the futures contacts, our condominium owner would be protected. This would net him close to $180,000. This would offset the $180,000 loss in the condominium's value because of the sale of the futures contracts.

Sell Futures Contracts

Contract Value	$61,037
Number of Contracts	× 3
Total Value	$183,111

Housing Prices Rise

If housing prices rise, the condominium owner loses the $30,000 in performance bonds, but the property is gaining in value to offset the $30,000 loss.

Who Is Using Housing Futures Contracts Now?

Stan Masucci is the CEO of Macro Securities Research, which is the New Jersey–based company that developed the housing futures contracts with the Chicago Mercantile Exchange. According to Mr. Masucci, he thinks that initially the most likely users of housing futures will be home builders who want to hedge the risk that the housing market will collapse. Perhaps mortgage lenders exposed to risks of loan defaults also will be interested.

Insurance Companies

Eventually, major insurance companies will offer the product to home owners. It will be marketed as home-equity insurance. The insurance companies will be using housing futures contracts to hedge their risk. Home owners would pay a fee for the insurance and not have to worry about understanding the complexities of the futures market.

Who do you think will sell the home owner this home-equity insurance? How about the home owner's insurance-licensed real estate agent? Who do you think will sell the sophisticated real estate investor housing futures contracts? How about the real estate agent of the future who is licensed in insurance and securities?

The Real Estate Buyer of the Future

The real estate buyer of the future will be the primary consumer represented by the real estate industry. Buyers in the future will sign buyer listing agreements as automatically as today's sellers sign seller listing agreements.

Buyer single agency will be the paradigm of the real estate industry. Any subagents will be subagents of the buyer's agent who may bring a property and the seller to the negotiating table. Dual agency will disappear. Divided agency will be nonexistent.

Commissions

We think the amount of commissions buyers in the future will agree to pay will increase to the point that sellers will not pay any real estate commissions. This will actually benefit buyers, sellers, and the real estate industry.

We have maintained in this book that buyers currently pay all the real estate commissions in a real estate transaction. We said this simply because the buyer is the party in the real estate transaction who has the down payment money and the ability to bring more money into the deal with new financing.

This book has been about having a buyer sign an exclusive buyer listing agreement. As part of your buyer listing presentation, we recommended you have the buyer agree to pay you, let's say, a 3 percent commission. This would be the typical commission you would receive through the seller's listing agent if you sold another company's seller listing.

4 Percent to 4.5 Percent Real Estate Commissions

We think the buyer in the future will agree to pay real estate commissions in the range of 4 percent to 4.5 percent to their buyer agent for full-service representation. We also think that buyers in the future will be amenable to paying real estate agents hourly consulting fees to assist the buyer in various aspects of a real estate purchase. And as a consultant to the buyer, the agent may or may not have a fiduciary relationship with the buyer.

No Seller Representation

As this is occurring, we think sellers will decline real estate agent representation. The exception would be the seller paying for hourly agent consulting on the various aspects of the real estate transaction the seller feels that the seller needs help. And as a consultant to the seller, the agent may or may not have a fiduciary relationship with the seller.

Cyberagent

We predict the number of buyers who will find their next home on the Internet to be 85 percent to 90 percent by 2025. As Internet listings become more sophisticated, we predict buyers will buy their next home the way they purchase items on eBay or similar Internet auction sites: sight unseen.

Your job as a buyer's agent is to become a cyberagent. You will look on all the Internet real estate auction sites to find that next home for your buyer. Seller homes will be auctioned either on the Internet or live or both! A growth area for real estate agents will be becoming licensed as auctioneers.

Buyer as Agent

As a final thought regarding the real estate buyer of the future, we introduce the idea of the buyer as real estate agent. With more and more information, education, and certification available on the Internet, we see a possible future in which a real estate buyer can become a licensed real estate agent online for one real estate purchase via a conditional real estate license.

Then there would be no professional buyer agent necessary. This is a scary thought. We wanted to address it now so that we as a real estate industry can insist that the requirements, education, training, and experience to be a licensed real estate agent in the future are at least as stringent as those for the person who cuts your hair! Even today, there are many real estate licensees who are not qualified to hold a license.

In many states, including California, it is possible to obtain a conditional real estate license by taking one college-level real estate class and passing the state real estate exam. Also, if a person has a four-year college degree, not necessarily in real estate or finance, the person can sit for the broker's exam. We as the real estate industry have to insist on higher standards as we move into the future.

What do you think the real estate industry of the future should look like? We invite you to participate in shaping that future at your local and state level. On the national level, each one of us is responsible for shaping the future of the real estate industry. Take your actions *now* to make the future you want a reality!

CONCLUSION

Congratulations on completing *Make Money as a Buyer's Agent: Double Your Commissions by Working with Real Estate Buyers.* We know you have a lot of material to digest. Our hope is that we have stimulated your interest in and understanding of why a new buyers paradigm is so important to your real estate career.

Our recommendation is for you to go back to the areas that are of most interest to you. Maybe you still are not clear that buyers are the party in the real estate transaction that have the money. Perhaps you want to go over how to ask for a retainer from a buyer. Reread those sections and then get started.

Our point is: Do something! Make some money in the normal real estate market by working professionally with buyers. If you are a lone ranger right now, you will not be for long once you start making money as a buyer's agent and word gets around. Seller's agents will hear about you and try to get their listings in front of your buyers! Get activated!

Pull a group of agents together and contact us for a seminar. You or the person in charge of your office training program can contact us for fee-based consulting and training. We are always coming up with more creative possibilities for making money, solving problems, and continuing education. Remember to watch for more of this Make Money with Your Real Estate License series. This book is the first in this new series.

We can be contacted through our publisher, written to at PO Box 274, Bedford, TX 76095-0274; or e-mailed at thetrustee@hotmail.com. Get out there and do something *now!* God bless y'all!

Chantal & Bill Carey

INDEX